THE SURVIVOR CHAMPION

THE REMARKABLE STORY OF A REFUGEE CHILD

JOSÉE KANA BIZIMANA

Grosvenor House
Publishing Limited

This book is published by
Grosvenor House Publishing Ltd
Link House
140 The Broadway, Tolworth, Surrey, KT6 7HT.
www.grosvenorhousepublishing.co.uk

Whilst all the events in this book are true, some names
have been changed to protect the privacy of some individuals.

A CIP record for this book
is available from the British Library

ISBN 978-1-83975-971-0
eBook ISBN 978-1-83975-972-7

PSALM 23: The Lord is My Shepherd

The Lord is my shepherd, I have everything I need.

He lets me rest in the field of green grass and leads me to quiet pools of fresh water.

He gives me new strength, he guides me in the right paths, as he has promised.

Even if I go through the darkness, I will not be afraid, Lord, for you are with me.

Your shepherd's rod and staff protect me.

DEDICATION

I dedicate this book to my children, my parents, my siblings, my dear uncle Sophonie Batwenga and all my dear family and friends.

Thank you for your love and support during this journey.

May God bless you.

CONTENTS

ABOUT THE AUTHOR

Kana Josée Bizimana (aka Josée) is originally from Burundi. She is a mother, humanitarian, and an entrepreneur.

She was born and raised in Rwanda and she now have Dutch citizenship. Her parents were refugees in Rwanda during the 1980s.

In the 1990s she was given the opportunity to visit her country of origin. She had a difficult time; war broke out in Burundi while she was there. It was a terrible experience living as a teenager in a war zone.

From the age of 13, she found herself travelling from country to country; running away because of the war, looking for a peaceful place. She lived in more than seven countries and learned first-hand about different cultures. This taught her how to live with different people, whatever their background, colour, or race.

At the age of 17, away from her parents in a strange world, she became the victim of emotional abuse. This helped her to develop into a strong and resilient woman, capable of handling any painful situation in the following years of her life.

She was born a refugee and spent all her life as a foreigner in different countries, so her only hope was to draw on her education. Her parents had always reminded her that wherever she was in the world, she should put education first. They had also grown up in exile, far from home, so they knew what they were talking about. Her father always told her: "Priority will always be given to the citizens of a country. Foreigners come second or third, and even then only when you have a valid qualification. So, put education first."

At the age of 26, after two disappointments in the relationships between her and the fathers of her children, she decided to raise her two children as a single mum. She wanted to give them her undivided love, to look after herself, to work on her passion, and focus on reaching her dreams.

Today, she can say that she is a happy and a proud mum!

INTRODUCTION

If you knew what I had been through, you would understand why I live my life to the fullest. Those who know a bit about my life story ask me how I manage to put a smile on my face, or how my brain still functions normally after all I have gone through. It's these questions that led me to write this book.

In the summer of 2010, I was in Belgium. I had gone to visit my friend Solange and I was sitting in her living room, relaxing on the couch, sipping a glass of orange juice. I was waiting for my girls to get ready before going out clubbing in Brussels. My brother Lambert was due to perform on stage in the club. I wasn't to know that within a few minutes I would be talking to someone, telling him the story of my life, and that he would say, "You need to write a book!"

When the doorbell rang, I went to open the door. It was my brother Lambert. He had come to pick me and the girls up. He was with our family friend Gilbert. I was in a black and yellow outfit, with my high heels on. I had just finished putting on my make-up.

"Wo! Wo! Wo!" my brother exclaimed. "Who looks beautiful?"

"Thanks," I said.

My brother went to the kitchen to fetch a beer from the fridge. On his way, he asked me, "Will you be driving when we come back from the club?" He came back holding two bottles of beer and handed one to Gilbert.

"Of course! That's my job, taking care of all of you after the club!"

Gilbert was standing beside the open window and trying to light his cigarette. I stood up from the couch and walked towards him. I asked him for some information about doing business in Kampala.

Gilbert became excited. "Sis, I know one day we will get there." He blew a cloud of cigarette smoke into the air.

"Of course, we will, bro!" I said, and we gave a high-five to each other.

I told him that I had been in a few other African countries, and that I also wanted to go to Uganda, especially Kampala.

"What other African countries?"

Before I could answer Gilbert, my phone rang. It was an international call from Zambia. My best friend Louise asked if I could send her the same perfume I wore when I went to her graduation in 2009. During our conversation, we used the local language spoken in Lusaka – Nyanja. I then hung up and went back to chatting with Gilbert.

"What was that language?" he asked.

"That was Nyanja, from Lusaka."

"How many countries have you been to and how many languages do you speak?" Gilbert asked.

I knew this was going to be a long story, so I walked to the kitchen to get him another beer. When I returned, I started telling him how I had lived in seven African countries and that I spoke the languages of all those countries. I told him how I was born a refugee, how I was bullied by my childhood friends because I was a refugee, how this all pushed my father to tell me about my origins earlier than he had planned. I shared how, at the age of 13, I was given the chance to go and visit my country of origin and meet my family for the first time, but war prevented me from knowing my extended family. I told him how I had survived civil wars in three different countries, how I became homeless after suffering emotional abuse as a teenager, how I survived domestic violence, and so much more.

During the entire time, Gilbert didn't even take even one sip of his bottle of beer. He looked surprised and sometimes confused.

"Wait a second!" he cried. "Am I watching a movie or what?" Then he paused before asking his next question. "Did you ever think about writing a book about your life story?" That was the moment the idea for this book was born.

By now my girls had finished getting ready to go to the club. Boy they looked hot! My sister Annie, who was holding a bottle of beer and trying to sip from it, looked like a model. Germaine, Gilbert's sister, was wearing a short dress and had her hair tight in a ponytail. Solange also had a short dress and her hair was running down her back. Seeing them all dressed up, I decided there was no time to lose. We left the house, our high heels tapping on the floor.

The next morning, having not touched a drop of alcohol, I drove the girls, my brother and Gilbert back to Solange's place. It was Sunday, 1 p.m., and my sister cooked chicken soup to kill the hangovers. I stayed in the bedroom trying to rest my weary head. As I looked up at the ceiling, I remembered the question Gilbert had asked me about writing my life story. Suddenly, I remembered a moment back in 2008 when I had been working in a restaurant as a waiter in the Netherlands. We were enjoying a staff Christmas dinner.

"Why do you say you are originally from Burundi when you were born in Rwanda?" my manager had asked.

"My father was 21 when he fled Burundi," I answered. "He had survived the civil war between the Hutus and Tutsis in 1972. He escaped from a load of dead people who were being transported in a big truck. Their bodies were going to be thrown in the river. The guards thought my father was also dead."

I had my manager's attention now!

"My father managed to jump from the vehicle and run away. Later he found his way to Zaire (now Democratic Republic of Congo - DRC). When he reached Zaire, he managed to go back to college. After college he went to the University of Lubumbashi where he graduated in 1977 with a Masters degree in History. It wasn't easy for him to get a good job in Zaire, so he decided to move to Rwanda. He had then married my mother who was also a refugee in Zaire, and in 1979 they decided to move to Rwanda. That's why I say I was born in Rwanda, but I'm originally from Burundi."

Every time I was asked where I came from, I kept telling the same story.

Even though writing was my passion, I never thought one day I would write the story of my life. At times I have had to go back to some sad and dark days and wipe the tears from my face. When that happened, I was glad to have my children and my sister by my side. In all of this I call myself 'a survivor champion' because of the journey I have taken; a journey of happiness, sorrow, adventures, and difficulties; a journey of travelling to many different places; a journey of changing villages, cities, and countries; a journey of crossing rivers, lakes, oceans, roads, and continents. Part of this journey I travelled with my family, walking days and nights, wondering where it would take me. I covered countless kilometres, in everything from cars to big trucks, small boats to big boats, even flying in a plane.

I spent days and nights within the sound of gunshot, and days and nights in complete silence, hiding in the bush and in forests, wondering if there was someone to rescue me. I walked quietly to avoid being heard by dangerous animals in the forest (lions, tigers, snakes). I crossed borders from one country to another, searching for a safe place. Some nights I couldn't sleep for fear of being strangled. When I at last thought I might enjoy my childhood, I became a war victim, and this prevented me from achieving the dreams I had dreamed for many years.

I believe things happen at the just right time. I knew that the idea of writing this book had been planted in my heart since 2010 but then something brought the seed to life. In 2013 I was watching the funeral of President Nelson Mandela. In one speech, the Former Tanzanian President, Mr Jakaya Kikwete, recalled how Mr Mandela used a Tanzanian's travel document to cross borders. I remembered how I had travelled through different countries with or without travel documents. I realized at that moment that my story could inspire others too.

I started to rewind the tape of my life story.

And I started writing the story you are about to read.

Chapter 1
THE REFUGEE CHILD

I was born on 15 March 1980 and named Bizimana Josée. In the society where I grew up, people say that when your first child is a girl, it's a sign of luck in the family. I was regarded as a blessing to my parents.

I was born at a place called Kibogora, a village in the former province of Rwanda called Cyangugu (now known as Western Province). One year and nine months later, another blessing arrived. My sister Annie was born on 26 December 1981. On 19 March 1984, there was another addition – my brother Lambert. Both my parents cared for me and my siblings. We had no cartoons to watch so my father was our entertainer. He was tall, very funny, and kind. I remember most of the nights my father would tell us funny stories, and we would fall asleep before he even finished telling the story. Although a caring person, my mum was stricter than my father. She used to cook delicious food for us. She was always organized and clean. She always took care of herself and I never saw her dress badly.

When it came to our education, my father was too soft, while my mother was very strict. My siblings and I have inherited something from both parents. We are all helpful and caring people, but one of us (my sister Annie) inherited our mother's strictness. My brother Lambert and I inherited our father's more tolerant nature. My time in Rwanda was a dream childhood. I basked in the total love of my parents. I enjoyed playing outside with my siblings and my childhood friends, and in great weather too.

I Want to Go to School!

It doesn't take long for a clever child to long to start school. I would cry when I saw other children walking to school wearing uniforms and I always wanted to follow them. I was 5 years old at the time. "I want to go to school like the other children!" I kept saying to my parents, bothering them to let me go.

Later my father was to tell me, "You were a smart girl and I could see it. That's why I didn't hesitate to let you start school at an early age."

In that society you could begin primary school at the age of 7, depending on the area you lived in. In my case, it was different. Kibogora was a small town. Methodist missionaries from the USA had helped to introduce some positive aspects of Western civilisation. It was a pleasant place with a great view of Lake Kivu. Far away you could see the IJWI Island, part of DRC.

There were two strong secondary schools, a good hospital where most of the doctors were from the USA, and a well-known Methodist Church. The Primary school I attended was also for the Methodist missionaries. It was called *Ecole Primaire de Kibogora* – Kibogora Primary School. There was also a preschool, but you had to pay extra money for that. To be in preschool, you had to be 6 years old. We started primary school at 7. However, I was 5 so my parents had to negotiate for me to be accepted.

My parents were both working at the time. My father was a teacher at the secondary school (the *Institut John Wesley de Kibogora*) and my mother was a teacher at the Kibogora Primary School. The school fees were not a big issue for them, so at the age of 5 I started preschool. A year later, in 1986, I began my first year at primary school. I was the youngest in the class, having started a year earlier than the other children.

I always had a soft and a big heart. I wanted to help other children and when I could not do something to assist them, I would feel like a loser.

I played outside in the sunshine, together with my childhood friends. We didn't have a lot of toys. We used to make them ourselves, coming up with new ideas for different games to play, sharing these ideas with the other children, and where they could find the materials for making their own toys. Sometimes we would receive a few toys from the USA brought by 'white missionaries' in the church.

We also had books, most of them written in English. Many had drawn images which you had to colour in. Reading those books was a very big challenge because no one among us children could understand English. We were in a country which was colonized by Belgium and where the international language was French. At our young age, even French was like a strange language.

In those days in Rwanda, at primary school all our lessons were taught in the national language which is Kinyarwanda. When we reached the fourth grade, we would start learning a few French words. At secondary school, we would take all our subjects in French.

We dreamed of living in the houses we saw in books. We would tell each other we would buy the same cars when we got older. They were built in the American style.

We used to say it was paradise; we had never seen houses like them before.

Preparing for the Future

I was brought up by Christian parents who taught us to pray, even though we were too young to understand the meaning and the value of prayer, we always prayed before we ate and when we went to bed. We had a prayer that we were taught in our Sunday school, and we sang it as our own prayer.

Our Christmas was celebrated in a Western way, taught to us by our missionaries. We would meet at the church on Christmas Eve and the missionaries would call out the name of a child to go and pick up his or her gift. I always had more gifts than I needed. I would feel sad to see other children going back home without a gift, their names having not been called out. I would take some of my gifts and hand these to them.

There were other children who didn't have the opportunity of celebrating Christmas as my siblings and I did. Some of us were lucky to receive books about Christmas, even if most of them were written in English. From these we learned ideas about how to create our own decorations, and how to decorate our Christmas trees.

I had a boyish nature. I always played with boys' toys and liked wearing shorts and trousers, which was unusual in our Christian society. However, if I played with boys and girls, I always played the role of being a mum, wanting to educate my children, shout at them, organize the house and plan. And that's me today! I am always organized and for that reason I don't lose things easily because I know where everything is! I like to see order everywhere. Sometimes when I tell my kids to organize their things, they get sick of me. But that's how they must learn to prepare for their future. That's my first priority and my highest duty – to teach them what's going to help them enjoy a better future.

Along with not having enough toys, we never had a specific place for children's activities. I was lucky to have a father who was talented and intellectual. He would create activities at home. He would organize something like drama and tell each of us children to act a certain role. Sometimes we would dance for him and he would sit and be our judge. When he looked at us, he would tell each of us what he thought we would become in the future. "I see an adventure girl in you Josée. I see a music star in you Lambert. I see an athlete or model in you Annie." And he was right. I have always liked adventure. My brother Lambert is now a rapper, and my sister has done some modelling.

I believe that parents can sense and see what their children will become.

Go Back to your Country!

I always liked playing with my friends outside. I remember how naughty I was when I always went out without letting my parents know. I liked going to my best friend Rachel, or to my other friend Dative whose house was closer to mine, and we would play until I forgot to go back home on time. My mother would beat me when I eventually returned.

In that culture, punishing a child by beating them was a normal thing. Later my father explained why. The habit of beating children became common after the colonial era – an era in which Westerners enforced slavery. The colonial slave-masters used to beat slaves as a punishment. However, my father never believed in doing this, so whenever he knew that I was going to be beaten, he would leave to avoid seeing me crying.

My sister Annie refused to go and play outside with me, so she stayed at home. She was scared that if she followed me, she would be beaten. So, most of the time, I took my brother Lambert who was very young (I am four years older than him). But then something started bothering me and I became confused – so much so that it reached the point where I needed to know the truth.

One day, when I was 7, I was playing outside with a few of my friends and we had a quarrel. I had a small football that my father had brought me from Zaire, when he had gone to visit his friends on his holidays. I decided to go home because it was evening and was getting dark.

"Can I borrow your ball?" my friend Eric asked.

"No. It's new."

Eric looked angry, as if I was refusing to give him something that belonged to him.

When I took my first step to go back home, Eric came and grabbed my ball and ran to his house.

"Give me my ball back! Give me my ball back!" I was screaming and shouting, running after Eric with tears pouring down my face.

Eric suddenly fell as I was chasing him and I fought to get my ball back while he was still lying on the ground. I then ran to my house with tears still on my face.

I didn't realize that Eric was following me until I heard his voice behind me:

"Tuzabirukana musubire iwanyu impunzi z'abarundi" he shouted in Kinyarwanda. (We will send you back to your country, you Burundian refugees!) His voice was serious and heavy in tone.

I had no idea what he was talking about. As I walked home, I asked myself, *Why did Eric say they were going to send me back to my country? Which country did he mean anyway?* I had no idea.

A few days later, I found myself outside playing again with my friends, including Eric. I had already forgotten about the argument.

"Let's go play in Simon's field," one of my friends said.

Simon was an old man who had a very big field with a lot of different types of fruit trees. We always went there to climb in the trees, sometimes stealing the fruit. It was the season for passion fruits at the time.

"Out of my field, you children!" a voice barked a few metres away from where we were playing in the field.

It was Simon!

"Nawe wa murundi w'impunzi, ndagusubiza iwanyu!" he shouted, pointing his finger at me.

Again? I said to myself.

Those were the same words I had heard from Eric, but this time it was an adult speaking them. Maybe it was an insult. I was angry as I stomped home. I was determined to know about my origins.

When I returned, my parents were not the only ones waiting for me. Our housekeeper was there too.

"What's wrong? Why are you angry?" our housekeeper asked me.

"Nothing!" I said, marching off to my bedroom where I fell asleep. I had planned to tell my parents what had happened and to ask them some questions, but I slept all night.

When I awoke, I didn't want to go and play outside before I had talked to my parents. Late in the afternoon, my father was in his office; I could hear him typing. Back in those days, computers were not yet popular in Africa. Most people used typewriters.

I knocked on my father's office door, but he couldn't hear because of his typing. I knew my father was a gentleman who never ignored his children, no matter how busy he was. He always welcomed a chance to talk to us. I always had things to ask about what goes on in the world.

I knocked again, but this time a bit harder.

"Yeah? Who's there?" my dad asked, still typing.

"It's me, Dad."

"Come in."

"What's wrong? You look sad."

I was scared and I didn't know where to start. "I just wanted to see you typing," I told him.

"Sit there. Maybe you can help me type a few words too."

I sat on a couch in my dad's office. He was concentrating on his work, not wanting to make a mistake and then have to use the correction fluid.

"Do you want to try typing a few letters?" he asked.

I jumped from the couch and rushed to his desk before he could change his mind.

He held my index finger and started typing each letter. I knew that the next day this would be the first thing to tell my friends outside. Children just love showing off!

"Papa, why do they keep telling me that they will send me back to my country? And what does refugee mean?"

"Who said this?"

I explained what had happened.

Dad took a sip from his glass of water, and he dropped the pen he was holding. Looking serious, he lifted me onto his lap.

"Listen," he said in a very grave tone. "Your original country is Burundi because that's where I come from. I was born in Burundi and so was your mother. But because of the war in 1972," he took a deep breath and paused a little bit before he continued, "I fled to Zaire and that's where I met your mother. She had also fled from Burundi. Then I heard I could find a better job in Rwanda. So, after we married, we decided to move here. We became refugees and that's why they call you a refugee too!"

My father lifted me from his lap and stood me on the floor. "Hold on a second," he said as he walked out of his office.

About five minutes later, he came back holding some papers. "See," he said. "These are your birth certificates. Yours, your sister's, and your brother's. Look here! It's written in brackets that you are refugees. And this shows that I am a refugee in this country."

He then pointed to some other names.

"These are your grandparents. My father's name is here – Kasa Bernard, and my mother's name is here – Bakura Cecile. And this is a picture of my brother, Batwenga Sophonie. We are the only two children born to our parents and we were all born in the village called Kibuye in Gitega Province."

"But what does refugee mean?" I asked.

"Being a refugee means that you live in a foreign country because you fled from a violent situation in your own country. In your case, it's different because you didn't experience any sort of violence or war, but because you are my child, you get the same status as mine and your mother's. It's one of this country's rules."

I kept looking at my birth certificate, paying careful attention to each letter written on it. Concentrating on the word 'refugee', I kept asking myself why it could be something that other children or even adults could use to make me angry or sad. I still couldn't get it.

"Are refugees bad people?"

"Not at all. And you know why? Because even Jesus was once a refugee and God loves refugees very much. So, anyone else who bullies you and says that you are a Burundian refugee, just tell them that you are a special person and that God loves you so much."

God Loves Refugees

I also asked my father why he named me Bizimana because other children used to tease me that I was related to a security man who was looking after local shops and schools – his name was Bizimana too. In that culture, people found that job disgusting.

"Let me explain everything to you," my father said. "You should be proud of your name. *Bizimana* means 'God knows'. *Imana* is a Kinyarwanda and Kirundi word meaning 'God'. And let me tell you why I gave you that name. That was actually the name that my parents gave me when I was born."

He pointed to the documents. "Look!" he said. "When I went to the university in Lubumbashi, most of our teachers were whites and they found my name difficult to pronounce. I decided to change it to a short name and called myself Kana. From that day, I was known by that name. I kept the Bizimana so I could give that name to my first child. That's what happened and that's why I told you that your name was special, because I gave it to my firstborn daughter. At first, I thought that I was going to give you my grandfather's name, but since I had given you the name Bizimana, I decided to give my grandfather's name – Matsiko – to your brother."

After my father had finished explaining everything to me, he also advised me that I should work hard in life so that I could go far. "When you are a foreigner in someone's country, all the best opportunities are given first to citizens of that country. Your turn comes second or third. So, you should work hard and be good at school because education is the key to success in life. Always ask me what you don't understand, and maybe one day you will get a chance to go and see where I was born and know where Burundi is." And that is how I found out that I wasn't a Rwandan citizen but a refugee there.

After this, I never felt angry when other children teased me or bullied me. Bullying is not something that heals after a short time. It's a scar that you live with. I used to feel bad when others bullied me, but there was something which I hated more – I knew that my parents came from Burundi and that they were refugees in

Rwanda. But I never liked it when, instead of saying my father's name, someone would introduce me saying, "This is the Murundi's child," meaning, 'This child belongs to that Burundi man.' I hated that.

In that culture, there was no system for therapy, no one you could go to talk to about being bullied. But I was lucky. I had smart parents who became my therapists.

When playing outside with my childhood friends, they would sometimes bully me again, but I always told them that I was a child of God and that God loves refugees.

My parents did their best to make us happy, especially by avoiding anything which could highlight the difference between us and other children who had a different status from ours.

I didn't know that our idyllic life was about to turn into long days of silence.

My mum and dad. Me in my mother's arms and
I was exactly 2 years old. The baby is my sister Annie,
she was three months old. (March 1982)

The three of us children with our mother.
My brother Lambert was three months old; I was
4 years old, and my sister Annie was 2 years old.
(June 1984)

Me and my sister Annie sitting in the front
yard of our house. I was 2 years and 9 months old,
and my sister was 1 years old.

Chapter 2
LONG DAYS OF SILENCE

At the end of November 1987, my father went away for a weekend, as he always did. I thought he was going for only two days, but two days turned into a week, then into two weeks, then a month, then two months.

Up until then, my father was the entertainer in our house and we couldn't spend more than two weeks without him. Now, for the first time, my father seemed to be taking an unusually long holiday.

The days passed by and we really started missing the jokes, the sound of the typing machine, and his tall, reassuring presence. My mother looked unhappy and discouraged. As for me, I didn't really know what was going on.

"Where's Dad?" I would ask my mother.

"He'll be back soon."

That would be it. I could see in her face she didn't want any more questions – another reason to be worried.

One evening, I heard my mother crying in her bedroom.

"Mum, are you sick?" I asked her.

"No, I was just praying. There's nothing wrong. Go back to your room."

A few weeks later, Mum took my sister Annie from our bedroom and she started sleeping with my mother.

I was now suspicious. Something was wrong, but I still had no answers to the questions racing through my mind.

Several months later, I was playing outside. As always, I took my brother with me. My sister was a mother's girl – she never liked playing outside that much. My brother was 4 years old and I used to tell him to come and play with the other children.

While outside, we argued about something that I don't really remember, and one of our friends got mad and started bullying me and my brother.

"Your father is a thief," he said, sticking his tongue out. "That's why he is in prison."

I felt humiliated and started defending myself, trying to pick a fight.

A few minutes later, I asked my brother if we could go back home. I was angry that I couldn't continue playing outside.

When I got home, I called for my mum.

"Yes," she replied. "What's wrong? Why do you and your brother look sad?"

"They just said that our father is a thief and that's why he is in prison." Then I added, "Is Papa in prison?"

Tears began to run down my mother's face. She took a long time to answer.

"No, he is not. And you shouldn't listen to what other children tell you."

From that moment, Mum started telling us not to play outside, but in our bedroom instead. Sometimes she locked the doors. That was hard because I always liked playing outside. I couldn't imagine being confined to the house.

Are we Moving?

Several months went by with my sister spending every night sleeping in my parent's bedroom. One day in the afternoon, I heard someone knocking on the door. My mum was having her afternoon nap. I opened the door and it was my auntie Julie (my mother's younger sister). She was holding a very big suitcase.

"Hallo Auntie." I gave her a full and loving embrace. It had been two years since I saw her last.

I ran and knocked on my mum's bedroom door. "Mama! Auntie Julie is here!" I cried.

My mother opened the door of her bedroom. She hugged her sister and they started crying. I wondered why there were so many tears. Was it because they had spent years without seeing each other? Maybe. But I was wrong.

Two days later I saw Mum and my auntie packing everything into moving boxes. By then my sister had joined me back in my bedroom. My auntie was sleeping with my mum.

Whenever we went outside to play, other children kept teasing us, taunting us that we were miserable because our father was in prison. The insults became so serious that I now had to know the truth from my mother.

I went home to tell her that we had been bullied again and that I was really unhappy with what the other children were saying about Dad. When I went into the house, however, the living room was full of moving boxes, bags and suitcases.

"Are we moving?" I asked my mother.

"Yes. And come here with me." My mother beckoned me to follow her into her bedroom.

"Sit here and listen to me carefully," she said.

"Your dad is in prison, but not because he stole something. It's hard for you to understand, but he is in prison because of politics. Whenever other children bully you again about your father, just leave them and come home."

Then she looked at me in the eyes.

"Be a good girl. Be responsible for your brother and sister and concentrate on your education, because you are the oldest and you have to make your father proud when he comes back."

"Was Dad handcuffed before they took him to prison?" I asked tearfully. I had just turned 8 years old.

"I wasn't there when they took him," my mother replied. "You remember he had gone for a weekend, right? That's when it happened."

My father was then sentenced to two years in prison and was locked up in the Kigali Central Prison, in the capital city of Rwanda. The prison is known as '1930' because it was built in that same year.

At the time, we lived in a house owned by the school where my father was a teacher. They had built some residential houses for teachers and we were renting one of them, but because Dad wasn't there any more, we had to move to an area where my mother could afford to rent a property on the income of a single parent.

Simeon, a friend of my father who was also a refugee in Rwanda, was doing theological studies in Kenya. He had started to build a house before he went abroad. Even though he had not finished building it, he let us move into his house.

My mother was still teaching at the primary school which I attended, and she couldn't afford to feed three children, nor pay the housekeeper and the rent on her own. She was a single parent now and making ends meet was a challenge.

Making the Best of Things

I really hated the new house – it had no electricity or running water and I had to make new friends in the area which I found challenging. The only friend I had was Stella and her family. They were also Burundian refugees in Kibogora. I only met my old friends once, and that was during our Sunday school. I cried and cried every day. I was struggling to get used to this new world, so different from the luxurious life we had before.

My mum started doing some business to help top up her income so that she could feed us and pay the rent and the bills. She and my auntie Julie – who stayed with us during the time my father was in jail – both started designing bedcovers. They also braided women's hair. This gave Mum some extra money to help during the hard times.

I remember the way Stella's mother used to visit every Sunday after church to check on my mother. She would encourage Mum to keep praying that one day my father would be released from prison and return to normal life. But my mother had lost hope. She now thought that it might take ages for my father to come back home.

Mum tried her best to take care of me, my sister Annie, and my brother Lambert. She didn't want us to think that because my father wasn't there that our lives were miserable. She always sent us on holiday, just like we used to before my father went to prison.

I remember she used to send us to a place called Ruheru, two hours walk from Kibogora. We didn't have a car, so we were used to walking long distances. Public transport didn't operate much in our area.

At Ruheru, there was one Burundian family I got to know. The father was a pastor of a Baptist church which was well known in that place. He had a wife and seven children – six sons and one daughter. His daughter's name was Jeanne Rose and I treated her as my older sister. I loved her because she always took care of me whenever I was at her house.

I would stay at Jeanne Rose's place for more than a week and most of the time with my sister Annie and my brother Lambert. Jeanne Rose would teach me how to cook. She was the one who taught me how to make pancakes.

Something else I enjoyed in Ruheru was watching them milking the cows. They did not have modern machines for this, so those herding the livestock used their hands. Sometimes I would hide as I wasn't allowed to watch. I would follow the cow herder to the field and observe the cows feeding themselves.

My mother would also arrange a visit during our long summer holidays to go to the capital city in Kigali to visit her cousins. That was when she would go and visit my father in prison. I only came to find this out years later. My mother didn't want to tell us she was seeing Dad. Children were not allowed to see prisoners.

I loved going to Kigali because it felt like a luxurious holiday. Some of the other children where we lived had never been in the capital city. The big city felt very advanced compared to our small town, which didn't feel nearly as civilized as the capital city.

My sister Annie and I played mostly with my cousin Florence. My brother Lambert teamed up with Florence's brother Fabrice. Whenever we were in Kigali, I also loved to go and visit my auntie whom we named Mama Gode. I would always come home with different kinds of toys because she worked in a nursery where they had toys from America and Europe. She would also keep her daughter, Marie Jeanne's clothes. When they didn't fit her anymore, she would give them to me.

These holidays had helped to distract me from the fact that our lives weren't the same without my father being at home. I enjoyed every minute while I was there.

February 1990. The day my father became a free man.
This was the day he was free to join his family after
2 years in Prison.

My father shaking hands with President Nelson
Mandela in Arusha during Burundi Peace negotiations.

Left is my father and right is my uncle Sophonie
(my father's brother). They were both in Arusha for
Burundi peace negotiations. (Arusha – Tanzania 2000)

Chapter 3
LEAVING HOME

It was February 1990, two years after my father had been sent to prison. I was almost 10 years old and in the fifth year of primary school. I was a student in my mother's class, so she was now my teacher. During one of the lessons, a little boy from a different class came and told my mum that there was a phone call for her in the headteacher's office. "Tell them I am coming. Give me just a second," my mother said. Either my mother wanted to finish the topic she was teaching, or she thought it was bad news, so she continued the lesson.

The boy came back again.

"Oh, I am sorry! I forgot!" My mum dropped the Maths book she had been holding and left to go the headteacher's office.

A few minutes later, she called me out of the classroom. "Jo! Come here for a minute!" My parents always abbreviated my name when calling me. My mum had a big smile on her face. I had no idea what she was going to tell me. "Your father is out of jail," she whispered.

I jumped to my feet, as if I was imitating Masai steps. I wanted to go and tell the whole world that I was going to be like any other child, living with Dad and Mum. But my mother gave me a sign to keep quiet. The rest of the week, I played outside with pride. I almost told my friends why, but I didn't want to disappoint my mother. It was hard for me to keep a secret for four days!

That weekend, my mother, myself and my two siblings, headed to the capital city of Kigali – a journey of about eight hours by bus. I don't think I will ever forget that day, running to hug my father after two years. My sister was speechless; she just kept looking at my father, trying to study him and figure out if he was real, while my brother burst into tears because he couldn't remember him. He looked scared to see a very tall man, dark in colour with long hair. My brother Lambert had only been 4 years old when my father went to jail.

To begin with, prisoners are released temporarily, for a period of three months in which they stay in temporary accommodation. During this time, the prisoners are allowed to go out but they have to be back at a certain time each day. After this probationary period, they are finally released. My mother had received a week of emergency holiday from her work, so we had to spend only one week with my father before they could release him to come home. It was a week of joy and I felt like I was in heaven. For my father, I think at times he was sad to see his children confused, not knowing what had happened to make him stay away from his family for so long. At the same time, he was overjoyed to be reunited with his family.

The Day Dad Came Home

I had a lot to ask my father, but I had to wait until he eventually came home. It was a Sunday afternoon. My mother and my auntie Julie were braiding their friend's hair. My sister Annie, my brother Lambert and I were playing under the avocado tree in our front yard.

Then I saw him. There was my father, stepping out of a car belonging to a man called Musoni. Our neighbour Musoni had given a lift to my father when he found him in the city of Kamembe. My father had been waiting for a minibus to bring him to Kibogora. Sadly, Musoni was later killed during the Rwandan genocide.

There were no mobile phones in those days, so we had no idea that he was returning that afternoon. It was the most wonderful surprise. We all ran and hugged Dad.

And there were surprises for my father too. When he saw our new home, he really didn't like it. This made him look for a job so that he could improve our living standards. He thought he would not be allowed to return to the school where he was teaching before he went to jail. But because he was so generous, social, and funny – especially with his students – the college invited him to teach there again. He was delighted to be offered a job straight away.

My father found it difficult living in an area where there was no electricity and no running water. He found it tough being far from the centre and far from everything, so after six months, we moved back to where we had lived before he went to jail.

At our new place, there was a great view of Lake Kivu. We could see large and small boats crossing the lake. And inside, the house had electricity and running water. We had returned to a life of luxury!

Why my Dad was sent to Prison

Before my father had been sent to prison, he had told me about my country of origin and from that time I knew who I was. Now I had more questions. I wanted to know why he had gone to prison. Had he been a thief, as the bullies had claimed?

One day during the summer holidays in August, I was sitting outside in the front yard with my father. It was late in the evening and the moon was glowing in the night sky.

"Papa, did you have bad food in prison?" I asked.

My father was looking up, trying to count the stars and at the same time trying to figure out the best way to answer me. "It was almost the same food every day," he said. "I hated it because I missed your mother's food a lot. You can't compare prison food with what we eat here at home."

"Did they handcuff you when you went to prison?"

"They always handcuff prisoners," he replied. "If they don't, they could escape."

"Where did they take you?"

"Into a very dark, locked police van," he answered.

I told him that I had cried when my friends told me that he was a thief.

"Let's go for a walk," my father said.

We walked down the street. Dad held my hand. "Listen," he said. "In Burundi, we have three different tribes. Hutu (84 per cent), Tutsi (15 per cent) and Twa (1 per cent). The Hutus and Tutsis became better known than the Twas. A long time ago, before the Europeans came to colonize our country, we were all one. We visited each other, married each other, we did everything together. At that time our nation was a single kingdom. The kings were mostly Tutsis and the army comprised both Hutus and Tutsis. This intermixing helped uniformity of ritual and language in the region and united the populace behind the king.

Hutu and Tutsi were at peace and we had no ethnic division."

I looked up at my father as he continued. "At first, Germany came to colonize us from 1899 to 1916. Then, from 1916 to 1962, Belgium took over. By that time Rwanda and Burundi were the same region, called Ruanda-Urundi. We even spoke the same language. It was after we all got independence that the names changed to Rwanda and Burundi, and we became two separate countries."

"What happened next?" I asked.

"Once the Belgians took over, they assumed from the differences in our physical appearances that there must be a division between us. They started measuring our height, nose, legs, feet, arms, they even counted our ribs. They concluded that those who were tall with long nose and legs were Tutsi. If you were short, or medium-sized, with a flat nose, they assumed you were Hutu."

My father paused for a moment while he took a breath. "The Belgian administrators believed that the Tutsis deserved the authority and power, and that the Hutus had to obey their rules and be their servants. This was the beginning of the division between Hutu and Tutsi."

I looked at my father. He was very tall – 1.98 metres to be precise. His feet were so large he had to order his shoes from Kenya or ask American missionaries to bring him shoes from the USA!

"Are you Tutsi, then?" I asked.

"My father was classified as Hutu. He wasn't very short. He was medium-sized, but he had married a very tall woman. In fact, my mother was as tall as me. My brother and I took after her."

"My mother had a mix of both Tutsi and Hutu blood. That was at a time when people from the two tribes were marrying each other, not caring about the differences. However, children from a mixed ethnic background are classified according to their father."

I was still a little confused.

"Your grandfather – my father's father – never believed in these divisions. He refused to be a slave of the Belgians, or anyone's servant. At that time, this was a brave stand. The Hutu were supposed to be the Tutsi's servants. That's why they were called the 'Muhutu'. Whenever the Tutsis ordered my grandfather to do something for the Belgian authorities, he refused. In fact, he was one of the people who would not give his land to the Belgian colony. They were always trying to find him to beat him, to force him to give them his land, but he would hide himself among his fellow Tutsis. He kept hold of all his land at Kibuye, his village, even after the end of the colony regime."

My father went on to explain that he never raised a hand to any of his children because he had seen how beating someone was so hurtful. He even told me that he was given a severe beating in 1972, before he could flee his country.

I was still curious about why my father was sent to prison. He told me he had been fighting for the equal rights of both tribes in his country, Burundi, and that he wasn't allowed to get involved in politics while living in exile in Rwanda.

"Ten years after Burundi had gained their independence," he said, "there was a tragedy in Burundi. It was 1972 and the Hutus wanted equal rights in a country ruled by the Tutsis, and where the majority of those who in the army were Tutsi."

My father sighed. "The Hutus started a fight in Rumonge and killed many Tutsis. Now the Tutsis wanted revenge and they started killing Hutus – educated people, high school and university students. I was 21 and a student at Athene Royale in Bujumbura. One day the soldiers came looking for all Hutu students, especially those who were more intelligent. They started beating them to the point they couldn't move. Others were killed. They took several hundred dead students and put them in a big truck to throw in the River Rusizi. I was one of those in the truck and they thought I was dead. I managed to jump and escape from the truck and run away. They didn't bother to follow me. And I simply ran, without knowing where I was going."

I gasped.

"When I hid in the bush, I found children who were fetching wood for cooking. One of them recognized me. The child told me that I had once given him sugar and sweets when he stood at the roadside, applauding me when I used to run the marathon. That child took me to his place and asked his parents to hide me. That family were Tutsis. They gave me a place to stay and helped me to flee the country to Zaire. By that time many Burundian Hutus had fled the country and were scattered in neighbouring countries."

I held my father's hand more tightly as he continued.

"And now you want to know why I was sent to prison?"

I nodded.

"I was arrested for having a meeting with some of my friends. We wanted to negotiate with the Burundi government to get them to accept having soldiers from mixed ethnic backgrounds in the army, so that those who were in exile could go back in their country. Not just Hutus, but Tutsis who were part of Hutu families, such as those who married each other. I wasn't allowed to have meetings like this while in exile in Rwanda. That's why I was sent to prison."

Mandela and my Father

It was 1990 when my father and I had this conversation and war had broken out in Rwanda. There were rumours of something called the RPF – the Rwanda Patriotic Front. This was made up of Tutsis who fled their country thirty years ago, who were hungry to come home, just as the Hutus who had for nineteen years been in exile in Burundi were. In Rwanda, a rebellion had been started by a militia composed of Tutsis who had fled their country in 1959. They had been formed to defend the rights of Rwandan refugees.

"I don't hate Tutsi people," my father continued. "That would mean me hating my friends or family members."

Then my father mentioned a name that I will keep to myself.

"You see your mother's cousin? She is from Tutsi descent. I can't hate her because she is part of my family."

My father insisted that he didn't hate people of a race or tribe. His goal was to fight those who didn't want to give him the right to live in his homeland. He wanted democracy for everyone, and he wanted equal rights for everyone.

"Think about Nelson Mandela," he said. "He was a freedom fighter for his country, South Africa. We are both fighters. They released me two weeks after Mandela was released."

I felt relieved after finding out why my father had gone to prison, even if I couldn't really understand the meaning of words like 'politics', or the story of our nation's ethnic history. What I did understand, was my father's passion.

"Love everyone, without division. If you're going to fight, only fight for your rights."

Now at last I knew that he wasn't a thief like my friends used to tell me. I was only 10 years old at the time, and it was only natural that I had thought he had been a thief. How was I to grasp that it was really because my father had been a 'politician'? I had learned about Nelson Mandela at school. I had not realized that my father was released the same month as Mandela.

Today I believe that children deserve to be told the truth. No matter how hurtful the truth could be, somewhere it will set someone free.

The Promise of a New Bedroom

Days went by and I was now enjoying my childhood to the fullest. My parents did their best to make me and my siblings happy and on 18 March 1991, I became a big sister again. My brother Deo was born.

I was in my sixth year of primary school. My father kept reminding me that I had to work hard and pass my exams so I could go to secondary school.

"Remember," he said. "I told you that you are a foreigner in this country, so you have to work harder. If your friends fail, they will get a chance to get even a cleaning job from their relatives, because this is their country and their home. They won't die from hunger. You understand what I mean?"

I nodded as if I understood.

"If you work hard and pass your exams to go to secondary school, I will give you your own bedroom."

I remember telling this to Rachel, one of my best friends, while we played outside at school on the playground.

"What?" Rachel cried.

"I am doing my best so that I can go to high school. I can't wait to get my own bedroom."

Kris, another friend, came and joined in with our conversation.

"I'm only interested in going to holiday clubs," Kris said. "And entertaining things like Drama and dancing stuff...."

"I like going to the movies," I added.

"I also like going to visit my grandparents," Kris said. "That's the only thing I really enjoy doing."

All I could think was that it wasn't easy or possible for me to visit the grandparents whom I had not met even once! My parents always told me that it wasn't yet safe for us to go and see them in Burundi.

When the day came for the announcement of my exam results, I was nervous.

It was June 1992 and there were butterflies flying around in my stomach.

"Congratulations! You have passed your exams," my teacher said.

"What?"

"Yes, you have passed! You will start your first year at secondary school in September!"

All I could think about was my new bedroom.

That was the only thing I really cared about at that moment!

The Day my Father Cried

My father was true to his word and I duly moved into a new bedroom. I loved secondary school and my father also allowed me to go to the holiday clubs and activities for students. My mum was a bit strict, but the good part was that my father always talked to me, advising me about how careful I had to be with boys. He trusted me, and I never wanted to disappoint him. I was Daddy's little girl.

During holidays, we watched movies on a big screen projector – movies brought by the white missionaries. These were mainly action movies, which was good because we didn't understand a word of them; they were all in English. We watched the images and listened to the dramatic music, the gunshots, and the screams. One of the films was *Rambo*!

The white missionaries had fine houses, and gardens with lovely flowers. We used to ask permission from the security guards to take pictures in their gardens. The place was called Mukizungu, meaning the 'white people's residence'. Most of them were pastors of our Free Methodist Church. Others were doctors at our local hospital and teachers at the colleges.

I always loved New Year's Eve. It was prepared by the local Burundian refugee community and those who could manage to reach Kibogora from other places, especially Cyangugu Province. Most of the time each family would cook a meal and bring it to share. We met each year at a different house. The hosts used to provide a room for us children and, when it was prayer-time, they would call us. They always asked God to help them so that one day they could return to their country and live in their homeland.

Sometime in the month of June 1993, I heard my father saying that Burundi was soon going to have presidential elections and that it would become a democratic country. On 10 July 1993, the FRODEBU party – Front for Democracy in Burundi – won the highest election points and we had a new president – Melchior Ndadaye – in Burundi. He was the first democratically elected and first Hutu president.

One afternoon during the August holidays, I was sitting in the front yard reading a novel. I saw a tall man, light in skin, carrying a big suitcase and walking toward our gate.

"Look at my daughter here!" the man said, looking at me, with a very big smile and a look of excitement on his face. He was confident, but I was lost. Who was this man, as tall as my father, who even looked like my father? I stood up, because we were taught to be polite to people, and I went to give him a hug like I would any other visitor.

"Are you not happy to see me?" he asked.

I stayed quiet and looked shy.

"I am your uncle, your father's younger brother."

At the mention of the word 'uncle', I burst into tears. My father had always told me how I looked like his brother. I had seen only few photos of him, but they were old and in black and white. He had gained a bit of weight compared to these old photos!

I gave my uncle a very big hug and smiled.

My mother was in the living room sowing some tablecloths as I ran to tell her. My uncle had surprised us; he had not sent even a letter to let us know that he was going to come to visit from Burundi.

My mum came running out and hugged my uncle. There was a lot of emotion on both faces.

"Run and tell your father," Mum cried. My father was round at his neighbour's place.

"Papa! Uncle Sophonie is at home!"

"Who?"

"Uncle Sophonie, your brother. He just arrived."

My father looked at me as if I was crazy. "Are you joking?" he kept asking as we hurried home. "Do you know how many years have passed without seeing my brother? I really can't believe this is true."

I had never seen my father cry, but that day I saw tears flowing on his face.

When we reached home, the two men hugged and hugged. My father and my uncle were the only children to their parents, and they had spent almost nineteen years without seeing each other. It was a good and unforgettable moment.

A little later I went to sit next to my uncle, trying to study him and I asked him if my grandparents were still alive and how many children he had. I was really curious to know about my other family that I had never met. He told me that he had seven children – two boys and five girls. Grandfather, I learned, was doing well but Grandmother was handicapped. She was very tall and had suffered a severe back injury when the house fell in on her. She couldn't walk very well, and she remained in bed, sleeping all the time.

"How tall is Grandma? Is she taller than my father?" I asked my uncle.

"She is very tall – almost 2 meters. Just like your father. Myself I am not that tall like them," my uncle replied.

A few minutes later, I had gone to tell the good news to my childhood friends. Of course, I had the right to show off, because they were in their country where they could see their family members as often as they wanted. It had always hurt when some of my friends told me that they had gone on holiday to see their grandparents. I used to feel so... so... bad.

During my uncle's visit, every time we sat at the table having lunch or dinner, my uncle kept saying that he was going to take me, my sister Annie, and my brother Lambert, back to Burundi. He kept telling my father that he had to let us go and see our grandparents before they died. He said that Burundi was safe.

"I am not sure about the situation in Burundi," my father said. "I still do not feel ready to visit or let any of my children to go there." He pushed his fork into his food, trying to finish the rice and vegetables on his plate.

My uncle took a sip from his glass of water. Then he leaned back on his chair and began to speak. "Listen, I think this is a good opportunity to come and see our parents and let the kids meet their grandparents. Actually, that was one of the big reasons why I planned this visit."

The only thing that scared me in what followed was hearing my uncle say that he would like us to go and live in Burundi. He said that he wanted us children to know our country better. He even suggested we could go and stay in Burundi forever.

"Are you not tired of being a refugee?" my uncle asked my father.

But my father's instincts were not to rush into any move to Burundi yet.

"You can come too. I will help you to get a job," my uncle said to my father.

"No way!" my father replied. "And I think I need a few days to think about you taking the kids. But if it ever happens, then you will take one child, or two. And I will have to discuss it with their mother first."

Getting Ready to Leave

I started telling my friends that I might leave them soon and maybe for good! I was proud that I was going to see the rest of my family – my grandpa, grandma, cousins, aunties, and uncles. I had only one grandpa left on my father's side. The two grandmas were still alive.

Several days before my uncle left to go back to Burundi, we were sitting at the dinner table one evening.

"The decision has been made," my father said. "We have decided to let one child go with you."

"Only one?" My uncle said. "And who is that one?"

"You are going with Annie and I will come two weeks after. I will bring Josée with me."

"Me?" I said.

"You, Josée."

It was all planned! I was going with my father to Burundi.

My father now had to apply for my travel document. This was instead of a passport, because we were refugees in Rwanda. He also needed to ask for some days off work.

The day after that, it seemed like the plan was now for my sister and I to stay for good in Burundi. I sensed this when I heard my uncle saying that he was going to start looking for a new school for me in Burundi.

Before my uncle left, my father called a family meeting. I was there, and so were my mother, my sister Annie and my brother Lambert. Our last-born, Deo, was 2 years old.

"Listen," my father said. "Annie, you are going with your uncle and I am coming later with your big sister Josée. This is not something permanent, because I am not feeling convinced to go and settle in Burundi. You two go first, and if the situation is manageable, then the rest of the family will join later. You deserve to know your grandparents, aunties, uncles, and cousins as your uncle has said. Don't think that we have abandoned you, because we will soon join you, or maybe you guys will come back if the situation is not good. Your mum and your brothers will have to stay here first until I figure out and plan for the new move."

I loved how gentle and professional my father was.

Now it began to sink in how serious it was about me leaving my friends and changing to a new school. I started getting nervous and even considered telling my father that I didn't want to go. But the thought of meeting the rest of my family and getting to know them meant that my excitement overcame my fears.

Three weeks after my uncle had left with my sister, my travel document was now ready. It was time for me to go to Burundi, to see my country of origin for the first time.

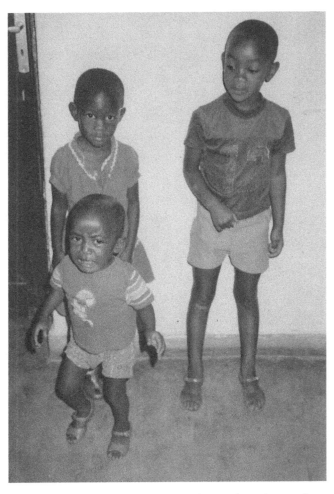

Me in shorts (I loved wearing shorts than dresses),
my sister Annie, and my brother Lambert crying because
he was always scared of the camera. In the society we
grew up, our parents shaved our hair until we finished
primary school. It was until we started secondary
school that we would start growing our hair.

With my Auntie Julie. At the left is my sister Annie, in the middle is my brother Lambert and me at the right. (1989)

My two childhood best friends in our school uniforms.
We were both in our first year of secondary school
in Rwanda. Left Josephine, in the middle Rachel
and me. (1992)

Chapter 4
TRAPPED IN A WAR ZONE

At 8 a.m. on 1 September 1993, we took the bus and headed to Kamembe, a small city in Cyangugu, where we boarded another bus headed to Ruhwa, on the border of Rwanda and Burundi. As I sat next to the window, looking outside, I saw one of my friends holding her books and walking to school. I waved at her, wondering if I was going to see her again, thinking about making new friends in a new country. I felt torn, but I took heart from the fact that I was going to fulfil a dream that I'd had all my life – of hearing my grandparents relating funny stories and being spoiled by my grandparents, aunties and uncles.

Late in the afternoon, we reached the border and my father handed our travel documents to the immigration officer. They stamped them and waved us on. After we crossed the Rwanda border and entered Burundi territory, I started hearing a language similar to what I spoke in Rwanda – Kinyarwanda.

"Why do people in Burundi speak like us in Rwanda?" I asked my father. Even though the accent was different, I could tell it was the same language.

"You remember I told you that before the colonial regime that Burundi and Rwanda were one region and we spoke the same language?" my father asked. "After we all got independence, the accent changed a bit, but we still understand each other." Actually, Kirundi and Kinyarwanda are like Dutch and Flemish.

After we crossed the border, we took a walk of almost two kilometres and climbed onto another bus which took us on a two-hour journey to Bujumbura, the capital city of Burundi. One of my father's old friends was waiting to pick us up. My father couldn't hide his emotions. It had been twenty-one years since he had left his country.

After a warm welcome, we walked to the car. My father, seeing a building just ahead, pointed to it. "See there?" he said to me. "That was my college before I left in 1972."

Then my father's friend asked if I was his first child.

"Yes. She is my firstborn. Her younger sister is already at my parent's village."

"At your village? How come?"

"My brother came to visit us a month ago in Rwanda and brought my daughter Annie back here with him."

Then my father turned to me. "Are you excited to be here?"

I didn't know how to answer.

"Anyway, you will get to know it better," my father said.

My father asked his friend if they could get something to drink before we hit the road to Kibuye-Bukirasazi, the village where he was born. Suddenly, hearing all the people speaking their language, it sank in that I really was in a new place. It wasn't a dream. I had so many questions running through my mind. *Does my grandfather look like that old man over there? When are we leaving?*

"Alright, let's get ready and head to the village," my father said, rolling up his shirt sleeves. We boarded a Toyota Carina and headed to Gitega Province. It was getting dark and I could no longer see the mountains. I was so tired I fell asleep.

I woke with a start.

"Jo!" my father called. "Wake up! We are almost there!"

I looked outside. It was very dark and all I could see were petrol lamps hanging outside the front of the small bars where local alcohol was sold.

We reached a place where the car could not pass, and we walked until we arrived at my grandparents' house. I was scared; it was very dark and there was no electricity. We had to use a torch along the unpaved road. It had been raining and the road was slippery.

As we walked slowly, I could make out lights ahead. We were close to my grandparent's house now.

"Hellooooo!" Suddenly people were shouting and came running towards me, reaching out, hugging, kissing.

I burst into tears.

Off to Boarding School

"Where's my granddaughter?" The voice was that of an old man talking to my father. I knew it was my grandfather.

"Bizimana," the old man said to my father. "Come here my son."

My father had once told me that he was given my name Bizimana when he was born. I felt happy and proud. Although it was not always the custom for a child to share their father's name, I did.

Peering into the darkness, I saw an old man, medium height, wearing a black short-sleeved shirt and trousers. He walked towards me and gave me a big hug, followed by a kiss on my cheek. He uttered many blessings over me and said a short prayer for me. It was the most wonderful feeling.

My grandfather asked me to follow him to the small house where Grandma was sleeping. Grandpa explained that Grandma stayed inside because she was sick. Grandpa held my hand, while with his other, he held a petrol lamp.

We entered the house.

"Here is Bizimana's daughter," Grandpa said, trying to lift his wife so that she could see me. The light was poor, so it was hard to make her out. My grandma held my hands, gave me blessings, and said that she was happy to see the grandchild from their firstborn son.

We all went to have dinner at my uncle's house, near my grandpa's small house. In the middle of the dinner, my uncle said that he had already arranged for me to go to my new school and that we were leaving early in the morning.

"School already?" I cried.

"Yes," my uncle said. "School started two weeks ago. So, you're behind."

The next morning, I asked if I could go and see my grandparents during the day because I had seen so little the night before in the poor lighting.

"Your grandpa has already left to go to the field," he said. "And Grandma will still be sleeping. For now, you must go and see your new school."

My uncle had registered me in a girl's boarding school called ENF – *Ecole Normale des Filles* (Girl's

Academic Secondary School). When we arrived, we had to talk to the headteacher and check if my place was still available. It was, but I was going to have to be one year behind because my level at French was poor compared to other students. In Burundi primary schools, most of the subjects were taught in French. In Rwanda, the lessons in primary school were taught in the local language – Kinyarwanda.

I was shocked when I heard this. I now wanted to go back to Rwanda and continue my studies there. I was disappointed, but I had no choice but to accept it.

"How about the uniforms and other stuff?" my father asked the headteacher.

"Your daughter can wear what she's wearing for a week. You can buy new clothes when you collect her at the weekend."

This was my first time in a boarding school and I realized that my father might be leaving me there, and that I wasn't going back to see my grandparents.

"Don't worry," he reassured me. "I know you are not happy about the school decision, but you will be fine. We just need to go and buy your school uniform, some useful equipment for the start – like books, pyjamas and other things. The rest you can get them at the weekend."

As we walked out from the headteacher's office, I saw a familiar face. A student was outside on their breaktime.

"Stella! Is that you?" I shouted.

She looked at me as if she was dreaming. We ran towards each other and hugged, both smiling and happy.

"Are you coming to this school?" Stella asked me. And before I could answer her, she crossed her fingers hoping that I would say a big "YES!"

Stella had been one of my best friends growing up in Rwanda. She and her family were refugees like us, but in 1989 they had moved to Kenya when her father began his theological studies. Later, when her father had finished his course, they decided to move to Burundi. I was so relieved that I had seen at least one of my old childhood friends at my new school. I mentioned to Stella that I was a bit angry that they had put me behind one year. She comforted me, saying that it had also happened to her.

Later in the afternoon, my father and I went downtown in the city of Gitega to get the necessary items to use until the next weekend. After we had finished shopping, he took me back to school. They showed me around the school and they offered me a bed and a locker in the dormitories. The dorms were organized according to the age and class, so I wasn't in the same one as Stella.

The President is Dead

Life in the boarding school wasn't as easy as I thought. I started missing my mother's food and my old friends. I was still waiting for the right time to go back and see my grandparents and my cousins. I wanted some quality time with my family to help me get used to my new life in a new country. At least I was with my friend Stella. She helped me to acclimatize to boarding school life.

Two weeks after I had started, my father came back to visit me and brought the rest of my school equipment. Before he left, he told me that the government had offered him a job as a general director looking after the cases of people returning from exile. A lot of people had started coming back to their homeland, since Burundi had become a democratic country. Most of them were Hutus who had fled the country in 1972. My father was now going to travel to Geneva in Switzerland on a mission, and he promised to come back and take me to visit my grandparents. The plan was that after six months, the rest of the family who had remained in Rwanda (my mum and my two brothers), could move to Burundi permanently.

On the morning of 21 October, while we were having our breakfast in the dining hall at school, some rumours were circulating that President Ndadaye Melchior had been assassinated. That was three months after he had won a democratic presidential election for the first time in Burundi. No one had yet confirmed the news.

We went into our classrooms as normal. While doing a French exercise in class, one of the students asked the teacher if the rumour was true.

"I know the same as you do. I'm not sure. We are trying to find out."

The next morning, the headteacher called a meeting for all students and confirmed that the president had been assassinated. She asked everyone to stay calm, until she had further information. I felt sick. I didn't know what was going to happen next.

The next day, before we went to our classrooms, the headteacher called another meeting and said that the security of the country was under threat, that in the capital city Bujumbura and in some other parts of the country, they had started killing people. Once again, she asked us to stay calm and be kind to one another. When I heard about the killings in Bujumbura, it was like a bullet in my heart.

I kept telling my friend Stella how scared and confused I was. She tried to tell me that everything was going to be okay. But as I was looking into her eyes, I could see that she was also scared.

That night, around midnight, we started hearing gunshots. Everyone was awake, and we all looked terrified.

"Stay calm please and don't go out of your dorms!" shouted the dormitory prefects. "Stay inside and turn off the lights!"

"Oh my God," I cried to myself. It was the first time in my life that I had heard gunshots and I felt nauseous. I kept going to the toilet. I was praying for God to speed up the night so that it could be the morning. But the shooting didn't end. The Civil War had begun.

The next morning, there were no classes, and everybody stayed in the dorms. I was confused; I was only thirteen and I didn't know what was going on. I started to regret agreeing to go to Burundi.

Late in the afternoon, we were ordered to go to the chapel to pray for the country. The chapel was outside the school, a five-minute walk away.

"The army was shooting people last night," someone said. "A number of people died!" another claimed. There were also some rumours that the army had killed a lot of people at my grandfather's village. My uncle Sophonie strongly believed in democracy and freedom. He would have been the first target. I started panicking that he might be one of those killed. The weight of this thought was too much for me and I collapsed. I was taken immediately to the headteacher's office.

"Are you okay? Are you okay?" people kept asking.

"Is she not the girl who came from Rwanda?" one of the teachers asked.

"Yes, she is the one," another teacher answered.

Later, I told my dorm prefect that I was scared and that I wanted to be in the same dorm with my friend Stella. That evening, I moved my stuff to Stella's dorm and we shared the same room.

Civil War Breaks Out

During the night of 26 October, the shooting started near our school. It lasted four hours, non-stop. *I am dying... I am dying...* I thought. People were screaming, women more than men. And children were crying.

My nights became sleepless and I cried every day, I didn't know if my sister was alive. She was at my grandparent's village.

This time it was civil war between Hutu and Tutsi. Both tribes defended themselves. They all wanted democracy, but the Hutus were angrier because the first Hutu president had just been killed. This time many Tutsis and Hutus died.

Was my father still alive? Was he back from his mission in Switzerland? My questions remained unanswered. I had no one to tell me if everyone was okay.

Three weeks later, Stella was summoned to the school reception. Before she could go to see what was going on, she asked me to stay in the room, and told me that she was coming back. A few minutes later, she did.

"A friend of my parents called Modeste has come to pick me up."

I shuddered.

"But I'm not leaving you behind."

We hurriedly packed a few things and left for Modeste's house in Magarama, in the centre of Gitega city.

On our way, I discovered that Modeste was a very good friend of my family and that she knew both my parents and my uncle Sophonie. Being curious, I asked her if she knew about the rumours that my uncle Sophonie and his all family were killed. Before she answered, she hesitated. I suspected things were not right.

"Tell me, Auntie." I called her Auntie out of respect.

"Err.... Erm ... I'm not sure. But people are saying your uncle has been killed with all the family. I am sorry."

My brain was a whirl and my heart was racing.

Stella and I spent a week at Modeste's place. We stayed inside the house. It was a nightmare. We kept hearing shootings right across the road from where we lived.

A week later, Stella's uncle Elias came to pick Stella up to go and join her parents. I went with them too. Once again, Stella didn't want to leave me behind.

As we walked to Stella's place, I became confused when we passed her house and took another direction. "Where are we going?" I asked Stella's uncle.

"To Stella's grandparents. Everyone has left Stella's village to hide in a safe place."

So, we went to Stella's grandparents, at a village called Ingwa.

Before we arrived, Stella's uncle said, "Listen guys, for your information, we don't sleep in the house during the night, because the killers come to kill at night. So, at 6 p.m. we start going to the bush. And we use different parts of the bush. If we sleep at one place one night, then the day after, we sleep at another place."

Oh God, why did I come to this country? I said to myself.

And that is what we did. We were eleven people in a small house belonging to Stella's grandparents – myself, Stella, her parents, her uncle, her two grandparents, and her five siblings.

The food became a problem, and we ate only once a day.

What a life! I thought.

I started to remember how my father had hesitated to let us go with my uncle. He had a bad feeling that something was going to turn out badly. As it happened, he was right.

Hiding in the Bush

One evening, while eating before we left to hide in the bush, the shooting started. I heard people screaming. "It's the army! Leave your houses! They are shooting!" We left everything and ran to hide in the bush a few kilometres from home. The shooting continued just a few meters from where we were hiding.

"Shh! Everyone quiet!" Stella's father said.

I had left in a hurry, without a coat or jumper and was shivering all over. I remembered the story my father told; how he spent nights sleeping in the bush and in forests before he could flee to Zaire in 1972.

In the place where we were hiding, there was another family who had a baby and the baby started crying.

"Can you please breastfeed your baby?" people whispered to the mother. Those who were shooting were around the corner, and they could hear the baby. The child kept crying, and we quickly left that place and went to hide in a big hole. That hole saved us.

A few minutes later, we heard shooting at the place where the baby was crying.

Then we heard screaming.

They had killed those we left there, including the woman and the baby.

"We know you are hiding here and we are coming to get you!" the killers shouted, threatening us. No one moved.

Later, we saw some lights further away – soldiers using torches, trying to find people hiding in the bush. We heard their footsteps and saw them passing near the big hole where we were crouching. I almost peed in my clothes. I was crying deep inside my heart. I asked God why I was suffering at the age of 13. I had come to Burundi to meet my family, but now my life was at risk. I was hiding and sleeping in the bush. I had left my room and a warm bed back in Rwanda. Now I was in a big hole – in every sense.

After we made sure that the killers had gone, we left and hid behind a big field of corn. We stayed there all night, and the next morning we went back home.

"Why is the army killing when they are supposed to protect us?" I asked Stella's father.

"They are looking for those who supported the president," he answered.

I couldn't get it. Why was I now living in a war zone, when I was supposed to be enjoying being with my family, especially my grandparents whom I dearly wanted to see? I was so confused.

Late in the afternoon, something strange happened. The shooting started during daylight hours, not in the usual time which was at night.

"Run! They are 1 kilometre away! And don't go where we hid yesterday because they know the place now!" The voice was a neighbour of Stella's grandpa.

We ran to the other big forest there, looking behind us to see if anyone was following. We hid there for three days. We had nothing to eat. It rained, and we had no shelter. We saw snakes slithering around us and all manner of forest animals. This is how I realized that God really protects refugees; we could have been eaten alive. A hungry snake doesn't leave you alive, a hungry lion doesn't either, so I was lucky. There were times over those days and nights, however, when I wished I was dead.

I started developing rashes on my body because of the dirt. Our diet was very restricted too; we only ate different types of fruit which grew in the forest. When I ate, I thought about how I could have been, right then, sitting at our dinner table back home in Rwanda, enjoying my mother's meals, or tucking into a lovely dessert.

Those three days were a nightmare. The army shot at people every day and night. One bullet landed in front of my legs. I could have been killed, there and then.

Three days later, a man among us left to see if it was safe for us to go back home. When he came back, he said we could go back to our houses. When we returned, we found the house empty, things scattered here and there. Even so, we weren't sure if we were really safe, so we went to sleep in the bush each night.

Time to Go Home

One afternoon at the beginning of December of the same year (1993), I was outside in the sunshine, trying to recover from a cold I had caught from the days and nights spent outside in the bush – I thought I had caught pneumonia but, thank God, I had not. Then I saw someone approaching the place where I was sitting. I gazed hard and saw a familiar face. It was my uncle Fidele (my mother's brother). *Let's hope he's coming to rescue me,* I said to myself as I ran to give him a hug.

"Tell me you are getting me out of here, Uncle," I said.

He laughed. "Don't worry. You are now safe."

"Safe? What do you mean safe? You can hear guns shooting any time from now... Stop telling me that I am safe. I just want to get out of here and go back to Rwanda." Tears were flowing down my face as I complained to him.

When I calmed down, I asked him, "How did you know I was here?"

He told me that he had first gone to my school, and they told him that I had left with Stella. Then he went to Stella's place and the neighbours told him that we had probably gone to Stella's grandparents.

"Start getting ready," my uncle said. "We must leave before it gets late. Remember the killing starts at night."

I told him that I had nothing to pack, that even the few clothes I had were gone when we came back from the bush. The rest of my stuff was at school.

Then I asked my uncle if he had any news about my father. I knew that my father had gone to Switzerland, but I didn't know if he was back or not. My uncle told me that my father was the one who had asked him to find me. The shootings had begun two days after he had returned from Geneva.

When I heard that my father was alive, I burst into tears. My uncle also told me that my father had fled the country and gone back to Rwanda.

Now I really felt like I was left in a strange country. The country I thought I had come to know, the country I thought was going to offer me what I had missed in my life, was now a dangerous and alien place. My new life was one of sleeping in the bush and in forests, dying from hunger and hearing gunshots.

I then wanted to know if my grandparents, my sister Annie and my uncle Sophonie were all alive, because it was rumoured that they had all been killed. Uncle Fidele told me that he also heard these rumours, but that people were telling different stories.

I was now really confused and lost. I didn't know what to believe. At least my father was still alive. But what about the rest of my family – the ones I didn't even get the chance to know?

I cried and cried. I thought about my grandparents in the dark house.

Oh Lord, why did you let these things happen?

An Old Woman Carrying Wood

Before I left Stella's grandparents, I said goodbye to everyone and I told them that I hoped to meet them one day alive. As my uncle and I walked up to the hill, I kept looking behind at Stella and her family watching and waving to us. I was waving back, hoping to see them again.

After we climbed the mountain, I could see the city of Gitega where we were heading. We were going there to get a minibus to take us to Bujumbura, the capital city.

My uncle started having doubts about the security on our way to Bujumbura and he told me that we might have to spend a night at my grandmother's place. This was my mother's mother. When we arrived at Gitega, my uncle went to ask the bus driver if it was safe.

The driver replied, "I can't promise you will be safe. Anything can happen, but I have to do my job. This minibus must be in Bujumbura for my boss. So, it's up you. Take a risk with us. Or, stay and travel during the day tomorrow."

My uncle Fidele decided that we should go and spend the night at my grandmother's village, Kibimba, where there had been a lot of killing. Tutsis died to a big number at my grandmother's village. As we headed there, it felt to me as if I was going to see her for the first time. My grandmother had come to visit us in Rwanda in 1985 when I was 5 years old, but I couldn't remember her face because I was so young. This time, I would remember her.

An hour later, we arrived. When we left the bus, I saw a young lady coming running toward where I was standing. She was waiting for my uncle to finish a conversation with an old friend. The lady looked so like my mother I thought that my mum had transformed into a young woman and come to rescue me.

"Hello Josée!" she said. "I am your Auntie Viola, your mother's younger sister. Your mother is our firstborn and I am the youngest."

Oh my God! This was the auntie my mother used to tell us about. If we had taken the minibus that afternoon, I would never have met her.

Seeing her niece for the first time, Auntie Viola hugged me tightly. I tried to give her a smile, but my mind was somewhere else, wondering if I was in danger. The place looked quiet and there were countless people around. As Auntie Viola, myself and Uncle Fidele walked along the street to Grandma's house, I asked if it was safe. My auntie assured me that it was, that they had stopped sleeping in the bush a week ago. She told me that they sometimes heard gunshots at night, but that didn't stop them sleeping.

My auntie kept telling me how happy my grandma would be to see me, her first grandchild.

"Did you know you were the first grandchild to your grandmother?" my auntie asked as she touched my hair, saying that she was going to make it look good. I had spent days in the bush; there had been no chance to take care of my hair.

As we approached my grandmother's house, I saw an old woman carrying wood on her head. It was my grandma. No one had told her I was coming. She knew I was in Burundi at a boarding school not very far from where she lived, so she had planned to come and visit me. But the war had prevented her.

When Auntie Viola called Grandma, she dropped the wood and ran to hug me.

"I thought you were going to die before I could meet you," she said. "Oh Lord, thank you for protecting my grandchild. Keep protecting her. Bless her and take her back safely to her parents in Rwanda."

I looked at her, trying to see if I could see any resemblance with my mum.

"You know what, Grandma?" I said. "You have the same toes and fingers as my mother."

She laughed and then said she was going to cook a nice meal for her grandchild.

I was excited in one part of my heart, but in another I was hurt that I didn't have a chance to see my other grandparents.

That night at my grandma's house passed safely. I slept like a baby and recovered from the sleepless nights that I had spent in the bush. I had not even realized that morning had broken the next day until I heard my auntie coming to wake me up for breakfast.

When I finished getting ready, my grandma prayed for a safe journey for us to Bujumbura. She said she wished to see me again in the future if God kept us alive, and that she wished me a safe journey back to Rwanda. She asked me to take care of my mother and that she wished to see her soon too. I rubbed my eyes trying not to let my tears fall on my face.

Then my uncle and I left and headed to Bujumbura.

The Letter from my Father

When we arrived, the city was full of armed soldiers and police officers. Everyone walked with fear on their faces.

I started asking my uncle when I was going to Rwanda. I was desperate to leave the war zone and go back to my parents, but my uncle told me that he didn't know exactly when I was going, because my father had to send someone to take me to Rwanda from Bujumbura. I was so disappointed that I had to spend more than a week in a country where I knew that any time I could be killed.

That first night in Bujumbura, I couldn't sleep. It was very hot and mosquitoes were biting me all over. I was still suffering from the rashes that appeared on my body while we slept outside in the forest and bush. I couldn't take it and I started crying. I said a short prayer and asked God to speed up the days until someone came to rescue me.

One week later, my uncle said that he wanted to take me to do some clothes shopping in the city.

"I don't want you to look miserable when you go back to Rwanda. You need proper clothes."

I had spent months with no proper diet, no clothes, no shower, so he really wanted to take care of me.

By then, someone was on their way to come and take me back to Rwanda. My father had contacted my uncle to let him know that I should get prepared and that person was going to be there within three days. My hope started to return. I knew the three days would go slowly. I just wished I could speed them up.

Two days later, I saw my uncle coming earlier than the time he used to come home from his work. He was with a guy that I did not recognize. Yet I sensed that I had seen him somewhere.

"My name is Denis," he said.

I must have looked confused.

"Don't you remember me spending a night at your place in Rwanda?"

As if I recorded everyone who spent days and months at our place! My parents welcomed a lot of people. Some spent days; others, months. A lot of them were homeless.

Denis reached into his backpack and handed me an envelope. "Here is your dad's letter."

I quickly opened the envelope.

"Yeah, this is my father's handwriting," I said.

Then I read the letter. My father told how he had sent someone to pick me up. He described what the guy looked like and he gave me a coded message to ask him to make sure that he was the right person.

Denis gave the right answer.

It was time to go home.

My daughter Lee Ann at 9 years old, and my son Lenny at 6 years old. (Netherlands, August 2010)

My son Lenny in the pram and my daughter Lee Ann
on the pram standing board. This was the easiest way
to transport my children if I wasn't using the bicycle.
(Netherlands, 2005)

Me and my daughter Lee Ann. A week after escaping
death when Peter wanted to burn me. This was
the bicycle I used to escape and run away.
(Netherlands - July 2002)

Chapter 5
THE ROAD TO RECOVERY

"Do you think I am a refugee now?" I asked. It was 20 December 1993, and I was travelling back to Rwanda. On the journey to Ruhwa, on the Rwanda-Burundi border, I had started talking with Denis.

"Why do you think that?" he asked.

"I'm fleeing from a war."

"So?"

"So, my father told me that a refugee is someone who flees from a country or a place where there is violence or war."

Denis sighed. "You shouldn't be going through such things at 13 years of age. You should be enjoying school."

When we reached the border, Denis had my travel documents stamped and we passed through both the Burundi and the Rwanda immigration control. As we walked to the bus for Kibogora, I saw someone I suspected was my father's friend, Steve.

"I thought you were dead!" he said. It turns out I was right; it was him. "We heard rumours that you and your sister were killed at your grandparent's place."

I shook my head.

Then he asked, "Is your father still alive?"

"Yes. He managed to get back to Rwanda."

Steve was a taxi driver and he offered us a ride.

"I don't want a fare," he said. "I'm giving back for the good things your parents have done for me." This was no small gesture. The journey was two-and-a-half hours long, but Steve considered it a small repayment for the kindnesses my parents had showed him when his wife had been sick.

I sat in the back seat looking through the window, watching people walking around and looking happy. Others were running businesses, such as women selling vegetables and fruits at the roadside. No one seemed worried about their security. It was all so different from the days and nights hiding in houses or in the bush. My heart broke.

As we were approaching Kibogora, I started to see familiar faces. Students had already started their Christmas holidays and I saw one of my former classmates. I hid my face. I don't know why, but I felt ashamed.

Finally, we arrived at my house.

I was home.

When I rushed through the gate, I saw my brother Lambert. He was playing outside. He had not seen me.

I called him.

At first, he thought he was dreaming and he rubbed his eyes.

Then he came running and hugged me, not wanting ever to let me go. He was so pleased to see me that he forgot to greet Denis and Steve.

Then he rushed off to tell my parents.

I was just bending down to pick up my small bag when I saw my parents racing towards me, tears pouring down their faces.

"Welcome home!" my mother cried, as she and my father hugged me.

My father was speechless. He kept looking at me. He couldn't believe that it was happening, that I was finally back.

It was a miracle to be back home and safe. God had protected me and saved me.

I went to take a shower and the rash that I had developed while sleeping outside in the bush, started itching. It hurt so badly, like all the painful memories of the war-torn place I had left behind.

Feelings of Shame

When I had finished my shower, my mother called to say that the food was ready on the table. Oh, how I had missed my mother's food!

"I hope you never have to go through what I have gone through," I said.

"Well, now you are safe," my mother said. "So, take advantage of it and eat your food."

We all laughed.

"I see you have rashes on your body," my father said, touching my arm.

I told them about hiding in the bush and sleeping all night there. Everyone at the table looked sad when they heard me tell of it.

My father said, "You relax for a few days and then we will talk. You don't have to talk about what happened. I know your heart is still broken and you want to tell us what happened. But wait until you are ready."

After dinner, we sat in the living room.

"Do you have any proof that Annie, my grandparents and Uncle Sophonie and his family have been killed?" I asked.

Before my father gave me an answer, he took a sip from his glass of wine. After a pause, he said, "Everyone here thought that you were dead. This turned out to be just a rumour. I am still doing my investigations about Annie and the others. I think we should all keep praying for them. I have a feeling she is still alive too, and the others."

Then my father asked me not to talk about anything regarding what had happened until after Christmas.

"See, it's Christmas in four days. It's time to rest," he said.

But I wasn't really interested in Christmas. I didn't even want to hear about the Christmas story. That night I dreamed about my time in Burundi and I kept seeing people running after me trying to kill me. I kept hearing gunshots. I couldn't sleep at all.

The next day, three of my old childhood friends came to see me at home. Our housekeeper came into the living room where I was watching TV and told me they were outside. I really didn't want to see anyone, but my friends were dying to see me and insisted I came out. I was still feeling ashamed. *What if they ask me if I enjoyed being with my grandparents? What will I tell them when they knew I had been so excited about seeing my family in Burundi?*

In the end, not wanting to upset them, I went out and I overcame my feelings of shame. I gave each of them a hug.

"We heard you were killed!" Rachel said.

"I was almost," I said.

"So, what happened in the war?" Kris asked.

I told them I wasn't ready to tell them and that even my father didn't want me to talk about it before Christmas was over.

"I'm also having nightmares," I concluded.

"Anyway," they said. "It's great that you are safe, and we are happy to see you back!"

"Thanks," I said.

"Are you joining school after the Christmas holidays?" Kris asked. "You still have your place there."

"I'll have to talk to my parents about that first," I replied. I didn't want to let on that in Burundi I had been put one year behind because of my poor knowledge of French. However, I did know that if I went back to school I would join them in the second grade of secondary school, where I was before I went to Burundi.

My Parents, the Therapists

On Christmas Day 1993, I refused to go to church with my parents. They begged me, but I wasn't in the mood. I was feeling down and, deep inside, I was still scared.

"Leave her," my father said. "She needs to recover from all the pain."

"It's okay," my mum said. "You can stay at home."

When my parents had left for church, I went into my bedroom and slept all day. I didn't wake up until 10 p.m. I was clearly catching up for all the sleepless days and nights during the war in Burundi.

It was a strange time. I can only compare it to being like when you have been many hours at a place with very loud music. When you find yourself in a quiet place afterwards, you still keep hearing the music in your brain. That's what happens when you have heard gunshots for so long. When you get to a safe place, it all comes back. I was only 13 years old and it was hard for me to cope. So, that Christmas Day, I took the opportunity and slept to the maximum.

One afternoon, four days after Christmas, my parents called me in to their bedroom.

"Do you think you can now tell us what happened to you?" my father asked.

"I think so."

My mother asked me to sit where they could look at me. I sat on the chair in their bedroom and I started to tell them everything. I told them how we had first heard about the awful things happening in the country when we went for breakfast at school. I told them about the time I collapsed when I heard that they had killed everyone at my father's village; and about spending most of our nights and days in the forest and the bush while I was with Stella's family. I told them how my heart was broken because I didn't get a chance to get to know my grandparents and my other family members. "I wish I had never gone there," I said.

My parents wiped the tears from their faces and came to hold me.

"It's okay," they said, "You are safe now."

"Is it okay?" I said. "Is it okay that my sister died? Is it okay that I only saw my grandparents and my cousins once, in the poor light of a petrol lamp? Is it okay that my uncle, my sister, my cousins, and my grandparents are all dead?"

"Listen," my father said. "Those are still rumours. I am hoping to get a true report very soon."

From that time, my parents became my therapists, especially my father, who took his time to talk to me and made sure that every conversation between us went smoothly. He didn't want to force me to do things that I didn't want to do, but he always stressed how important some things were, especially my education. He was scared that I was going to refuse to go back to school, so he started to insist that in January 1994, I would return. "Education has to come first," he kept saying.

"But I'm afraid I will fail and be laughed at," I protested.

"That's why I have arranged for someone to give you after-school lessons so that you can catch up with the things you missed. I trust you. I know you are going to make it."

Good News and Bad News

From that time, I started asking myself who was to blame for all that I'd gone through. Was it my uncle? He had come to visit us and had asked my father to let us go and see our family. He had been the one who wanted us to see our country of origin. If it wasn't him, was it my father? He was the one who agreed to it.

In the end, I realized that none of them was to blame. My uncle wanted the best for us, and so did my father. None of them knew that there was going to be a war. Even my father had wanted to see his parents after twenty-one years in exile.

In January 1994, I went back to school and returned to where I had been before I left for Burundi. Three weeks later, my father called a family meeting.

My mum, my brother Lambert and I went into the living room.

"I have something to tell you." My heart missed a beat. I was so scared.

"Close the door behind you," my father asked Lambert to close the front door. It was very warm outside. The sun was beating down. It was a windless day. That's when I knew something was wrong.

"Well, I have some news. Good news and bad news." I shuddered.

"The good is that Annie is still alive!"

I was so excited I gave a high-five to my brother.

"There's more," my father said when we had calmed down. "Uncle Sophonie and all his seven children are also still alive!"

Another high-five for my brother.

My father leaned back on the sofa, paused, and then looked up. I could see he was trying to hold back his tears.

"Your grandparents, your uncle's wife and one of your cousins have been killed."

Hearing this, we all started to cry.

"I'm afraid this is 100 per cent true," my father added.

I wept like I had never wept before.

I will never forget that day.

When Annie Came Home

My sister and my cousins (my uncle's children) were still in Burundi at a place called Kumoso, near the Tanzanian border. My uncle Sophonie had also managed to flee and reach Tanzania. The next step was to look for someone who could pick up my sister. Two weeks later, a guy called John Peter agreed to go and bring Annie back home.

One afternoon in the middle of February, when I had started recovering from my rashes, I had gone outside. Three of my friends – Rachel, Kris, Josephine – and I sat on a bench by the roadside, where we could see people passing. Now, feeling more confident, I was trying to tell them about my experience of the war in Burundi.

"You know when we saw you," Kris said, "We thought we had seen a ghost."

We all laughed.

"To be honest," Josephine added, "Everyone thought you were dead."

"I know," I said. "That's what I thought about my sister too. Everyone said she was dead."

"Is she okay?" Rachel asked. "When is she coming home?"

"We are expecting her this week – tomorrow, maybe."

While we were chatting and laughing about silly things, I saw a guy in the distance holding a small bag. There was a young girl beside him.

The young girl started running towards me.

When I looked more carefully, I could see who it was. It was Annie!

She had recognized me from afar, but I had not. She was skinnier than before, and her hair was longer and darker.

I stood up, ran towards her, then we were in each other's arms, the tears flowing from our eyes. My friends joined in too.

"Oh my God!" I cried out to my sister. "You have changed so much."

As I looked at her, I knew without any words being said that she had gone through the same ordeal as me, maybe worse. She looked so miserable.

I thanked John Peter and told my friends I would see them the next day at school. I held my sister's hand and we walked home together. No one knew that Annie was coming home that day. None of us had mobile phones.

As we walked through the gate, everyone was sitting in the front yard in the sunshine. When Annie saw them, she rushed to give them hug. My parents hugged her tightly, overjoyed to see all their children home and safe.

Annie's Terrible Story

We were all dying to know about what happened to all our family members back in Burundi. But my father didn't want to ask my sister about anything before she had first had time to rest and recover, just as I had.

My sister looked more traumatized than me. She didn't want to go outside. She was scared to talk to anyone because her accent had changed. She spoke more Kirundi than Kinyarwanda. She thought that everyone was going laugh at her. I could understand her feelings; I had also been ashamed when I came back.

A week later, my parents did the same thing they had done with me. This time it was more serious because my father wanted to know how his parents had been killed. We all sat in the living room. "Are you sure you want to tell us?" my father asked. I really liked the way my father never wanted to rush into asking us what had happened to us during the war. He always respected our feelings and wanted to take things slowly. He probably didn't want us to have to relive all the bad memories.

My sister was ready, so she told the story.

"One night, a week after they had announced that the president was killed, we heard the gunshots which lasted all night. The next day, around 11 a.m., when auntie (uncle Sophonie's wife) was busy preparing for lunch, we saw some men fully armed and in army uniforms running towards where we sat in the front yard. They were trying to cover the whole place, preventing any of us from escaping. I heard my cousin Richard saying, 'Run, and don't go inside! Run! They are coming with guns.' Grandpa was preparing to go to the field and cut the trees. He had a machete in his hands. Me and my cousin Jane ran and went into Grandpa's house, and we hid under the bed where Grandma was sleeping.

I didn't know whether others had managed to flee or not. I heard the killers saying: 'Come out from the house, we know you are hiding there.' I didn't know if they were threatening us, so when I wanted to come out, my cousin Jane stopped me. She pulled me back under the bed where we hid and told me to stay put.

Then I heard other killers outside speaking to Auntie. 'Give us money or we will kill you.'

'I don't have money! Look! I don't have any money with me!' I heard her cry.

'Where is your husband?' they asked. If you don't tell us where your husband is, then we will kill you.'

'I don't know where he is! Please don't kill me!' My auntie was crying now.

Later, after maybe fifteen minutes, I heard someone saying, 'Kill that Hutu old man and use that machete he is holding.' They were talking about Grandpa. A few minutes later, I heard Grandpa screaming and I knew that they had killed him."

My sister paused when she saw tears on my father's face. I also burst into tears, remembering the prayer that my grandpa had said to me, the way he took my hand and showed me where Grandma was sleeping in their small house. It was all so sad.

After a while, my father asked my sister to continue.

"We could hear that Uncle's big house was on fire and that they were burning it down. I started getting scared that they would burn the house where I was hiding under the bed with my cousin Jane.

Two killers came into the house.

'Kill this old woman too!' They said. 'Kill her now!'

They kept arguing about killing my grandma. I was shivering, scared that they would look under the bed.

I heard one of them saying, 'Give me that bayonet! I'll show you what to do.'

Grandma screamed and then I heard her taking her last breath."

None of us could contain our tears when we heard this.

Then my sister continued. "About thirty minutes later, we heard no one talking outside, not even a bird was making any noise. Jane and I decided to come out from under Grandma's bed. Jane went to see if it was safe. After she could see it was all clear, she called me. I came out from Grandma's house. I didn't even want to look at her body because I was scared. But when I came out of the door, I found my grandpa's body lying on the ground in the front yard. He had blood all over him. They had killed him using the machete because I saw it covered in blood beside him, and my uncle's house was still burning.

While we were escaping, me and my cousin Jane saw one crazy man who had a mental illness and who was known in our grandparent's village as a sick man. He called me and my cousin Jane and took us to where others were hiding in the bush. When we got there, my other six cousins were all there.

No one knew what had happened to my auntie. But later, when we went to hide at another safe place, we heard that the army used a bayonet to try and kill her. She didn't die straight away but died later when Uncle Sophonie was trying to operate on her. She had lost a lot of blood, so she couldn't make it.

They used bayonets to kill people. They even tried to kill my cousin Perfect using the bayonet, but he didn't die. He has a scar in his shoulder to this day."

"And where was your uncle?" my father asked, referring to his brother.

"He was at work at the hospital. After Auntie died, the killers went to the hospital to look for him. They killed people in the hospital who refused to say if they'd seen Dr Sophonie. My uncle was hiding in a wardrobe in one of the operating rooms. After the killers had killed a lot of people mostly Hutus, my uncle found a way to flee the country.

My cousins and I also managed to flee. We spent days and nights walking. We never slept in the house. We slept in the bush until we reached Kumoso where a friend of Grandpa gave us a place to stay. To eat, we had to go work in the field, otherwise there was no food for us. That's where we heard that Uncle Sophonie had managed to escape and had reached Tanzania."

My sister paused and then concluded, "That is how things happened."

Returning to Normal

My father was deeply touched to hear about the death of his parents, how his brother had lost his wife, and how his brother's children had been suffering. He decided to send John Peter, the guy who had brought my sister back home, to go and bring four of his brother's children. He was even planning for my uncle to come and live in Rwanda. Uncle Sophonie was a very gifted surgeon at Gitega Hospital in Burundi. He had completed his studies in the USA. My father was determined to find a good job for him at our local hospital in Kibogora.

In the middle of March, a few days after my fourteenth birthday, four of my cousins – Violete (my uncle's firstborn), Mediatrice (the fifth child), Perfect (the sixth), and Willene (the seventh) – managed to get to Rwanda and came to stay at our place. Willene was the youngest. She was only 1 year old. Her mother had been killed when she was 9 months old.

As the days went by, things seemed to be returning to normal. We all went to school and tried to recover from the bad memories of the war. Sometimes we sat in one of the bedrooms and each one of us tried to recount how we had escaped death, how we had spent days and nights sleeping outside in the bush with animals. My brother Lambert was there with us, but he had no idea about what we were talking about. To him, it sounded like a movie.

One time my father found us in the middle of a conversation. He sat with us and started to tell us about how in 1972 he had fled from Bujumbura to Zaire.

"You see, we have the same story. I also spent days and nights in the bush before I could get to Zaire. But thank God, you are all alive. I just want you guys to concentrate now on your education. This is the key to success for all of you. Look at me, if I had not put all the effort into my education, I could have ended up being an animal hunter."

"An animal hunter?" we all laughed.

"Yes, an animal hunter! You know, when you are a refugee or a foreigner in a country, all you need to do is get a good education. Even if people don't offer you a job, you can always start your own business, just so long as you went to school and know how to put numbers together."

My father then paused and looked at all of us. "That's why I always tell you to take your education seriously," he said.

My sister Annie and me. Few months after
we left Adam's place. We were dancing with
joy celebrating our freedom.

At the front my sister Annie, and me at the back.
Even though I had a smile on my face, we were living
a miserable life. Here, we were at the roadside selling
bread (buns) for Adam. We were forbidden from wearing
our own clothes. Adam and his wife bought us those
clothes we had on. My parents always cried every
time they looked at this picture because we looked
unhealthy. (Zambia – Lusaka July 1998)

Me, my brother, and my sister at Durban beach. I was relieved after telling them that I was pregnant.

Chapter 6
IN THE MIDST OF A GENOCIDE

When my father travelled to Kigali to meet with someone who had agreed to drive my uncle Sophonie and three of his children to Rwanda, he had no idea that the storm clouds were gathering. It was 1 April 1994, and my father had arranged to meet the businessman in question and fix the date to chauffeur my uncle and my cousins. "I will be back within a week," my father had said.

Five days later, my mother was watching the evening news on TV. I was passing the living room to fetch something from the kitchen.

"Oh my God," my mother said. "We are in trouble."

"What do you mean, Mum?" I asked.

"I am not sure," she answered. "I just heard on the news that the presidential plane has crashed, and that the president was on board."

"What?" I cried, panic rising. I was about to go and tell my cousins and siblings in the other room, when my mum told me not to scare them.

I sat with my mum, waiting to hear if the news would be repeated after the headlines. After a few minutes, the newsreader said that the presidential plane had been shot down and that President Habyarimana Juvenal had been in the plane.

"Not again," I sighed. "Not another war." I was shivering so badly I almost peed myself.

I hurried to tell my siblings and my cousins what I had heard. "What? Oh Lord, not again!" my cousin Violette said.

We were still recovering from what we had experienced in Burundi and now this. We all went to bed and tried not to think about it.

Next day, the news was confirmed that the president had died, along with the Burundi president, Cyprien Ntaryamira, who was travelling in the same plane. They were returning from Tanzania after peace negotiations with the RPF.

For the rest of the day, nothing untoward happened. Then, at 3 a.m. on 8 April, we heard people screaming, especially children.

"We are dying! We are dying! Please don't kill me! Please don't kill me!" Different voices. Children crying. People pleading. We had no idea what was going on but we were scared. No one could go outside. Worse still, my father wasn't home yet.

"Stay inside!" said my mother, while trying to open the door and look outside to see where the screaming was coming from. It was our neighbour's house. "Stay inside! Go back to your bedrooms and switch the lights off," she said.

I was shivering. I felt like I wanted to throw up. We went into our bedrooms, but we couldn't sleep. We kept hearing noises – people screaming, things being broken – but still we didn't know what was happening.

Later in the morning, when my mother went to ask what had happened, she found out that our neighbour's house had been attacked by people wearing masks.

I remembered how, in Burundi, things started getting worse two days after the president was killed. I was speechless. I didn't want to go through the same kind of tragedy I had left behind just three months ago.

Singing and Blowing Whistles

On Sunday the 10th, we came back from church and sat at the dining table having our lunch. At around 1 p.m., we heard people with whistles. When we looked through the window, we saw young boys, adults, and old men running, each one of them holding machetes and wooden sticks with hard, heavy heads. They were singing songs and blowing whistles. They had formed a militia group called the Interahamwe (which means 'fighting together').

"This is dangerous," my mother said, while trying to pull the curtains closed. "I need you to stay inside," she added. I leaned forward and placed my forehead in my hands. *Am I going to survive a new war?* I wondered.

The Rwandan genocide had truly begun. Hutus were killing Tutsis everywhere. People from outside the area where we lived were coming in to join those who were killing people in our region. We kept hearing on the news that all over the country people were being killed. My mother had said we couldn't even peek through the window, but I sometimes did. One time when I looked outside, I saw a young man holding the severed head of a lady on a very long bamboo pole covered in blood. I will never forget that image. From that day on, I never slept peacefully during the genocide.

After the slaughter had been going on for about a month, we heard someone knocking on the front door one evening. Everyone looked scared. Maybe people suspected that we were hiding someone inside our house. My mother went to look through the window. Her face changed from fear to joy. "It's your father!" she cried.

We all hugged our father. It was as if our hero had finally come home.

My father looked tired. On his way home, he had seen worse things than we had. "It's terrible," he said, trying to relax on the sofa after the journey from Kigali. The journey was supposed to take eight hours. My father had spent more than eighteen on the road to Kibogora. He had been stopped more than ten times because of his physical appearance.

"The road is full of roadblocks," he said. "The Interahamwe are searching cars, even if there are no Tutsis in them escaping."

He sighed.

"Being tall in this country is now a crime. I had to show my papers to prove to the Interahamwe that I was a Burundian refugee"

Then he began to look angry.

"What are these American and European people doing here? I mean these UN and French troops. Are they not supposed to protect people? We need to leave this country. It's so dangerous. As soon as possible." Two weeks after my father had come back home, he started planning how we would escape to Zaire.

We will Finish you Too

One morning at about 9 a.m., a group of four Burundian boys aged between 20 and 24 arrived at our house.

They were students at the school where my father was a teacher. Their names were Kevin, Elson, Apollo, and Bonny. They were terrified.

"What's wrong?" my father asked.

"We were being followed by a group of Interahamwe who wanted to force us to join the militia group and help them to search for more Tutsis."

My father was very well-respected in the area, especially by most Burundian people in Kibogora, which is why the boys came to tell my father what was happening.

By that time, the Interahamwe had started searching in the bushes and in peoples' houses, suspecting that they were hiding Tutsis. In the process, they were recruiting more people to join them in that operation.

A few minutes later, a group of Interahamwe arrived and told my father that the four Burundian boys needed to show their support.

"Don't ever involve Burundian people in killing Tutsis in Rwanda," my father said to the men who were now standing in our front yard. We children watched everything through the window, since we were not allowed to go outside.

"We are Burundian, not Rwandan," my father added.

"How can a Hutu who fled from Burundi because of the Tutsis dare to say that?" one of the killers asked.

"I fled only from my enemies," my father said. He told them that even if he had fled from a country ruled by Tutsis, that didn't mean he supported the killing of the entire Tutsi race. His anger had been towards a government, not towards a race.

"Dore ibyitso byabarundi!" one of them said to the others, meaning, 'look at the Burundian who works with the Tutsi!' The word 'ibyitso' means 'people who work secretly with the opposite race'.

"When we finish our operation, we will come to finish you too," one of the killers said to my father and the boys.

Later my father turned to the four Burundian boys. "You guys should leave this country because that's what I am going to do right now."

Blood Everywhere

That same day, my father and another Burundian pastor called Mike saved a young lady's life. They stepped in and told the Interahamwe that if they killed the girl, that they would be killing a Burundian. Her name was Samanta. Her father was a Burundian man from Tutsi descent, but her mother was a Tutsi - Rwandan. "This girl is a Burundian. We have already warned you not to involve Burundians in the Rwanda situation," my father told them.

Samanta was spared and Pastor Mike took the girl to live at his place with his own family.

Another day I had a toothache so terrible that I had to be taken to the dentist. This was the first time I had come out of the house since the killing had started. I could see blood all over the place when my mum and I walked to the dentist. I became more traumatized and scared. Everything reminded me of the tragedy I had experienced in Burundi.

Even though it was the Tutsis who were mostly being killed, moderate Hutus were also murdered, as well as Hutus who had married Tutsis. Others were killed simply because they looked like Tutsis.

By then, I knew that my father was a man of quick actions and that he was organising for us to flee from the country. We had nothing to lose. During all those years my parents had lived in Rwanda, they had never thought of building or buying a house. They always hoped to go back to their homeland one day. This meant we only had to leave with the things we could manage to pack. We all knew that if Dad had said we had to leave the country as soon as possible, he meant it. My father wanted to protect us – especially my sister, my cousins and me. He knew we had seen a lot during the 1993 civil war in Burundi. It was too much for him to think of us experiencing two different types of violence in two different countries and in such a short time. We had barely recovered from what we had seen in Burundi.

The day came when he told us that he had found a small fishing boat to take us to Zaire. It was the beginning of June and he located a vessel to take us to an island called Ijwi. Ijwi is located in the South Kivu – Congo. The boat was going to leave the next day at 10 p.m. and we only had twenty-four hours to pack.

By 6 p.m. the next day, we had finished packing everything that we could take with us. By 8 p.m. we had finished putting everything in the van which was going to take us to the lake where the boat was waiting. There was not enough space for every one of us to fit in one van, so we had to walk in silence down to Lake Kivu. The road was dangerous, so we removed our shoes to avoid making noises. As we walked, we saw dry blood all over the place, even bricks covered in blood. Those bricks had been used to kill people. This is a picture I'll never get out of my mind. It all took me back to Burundi where we walked in silence when we used to go and sleep in the bush.

Maybe I was born to suffer, I thought. I was clearly not born to enjoy the same relaxing night's sleep as other children of my age around the world.

When I think back now, I realize that there are people who were born the same day as me, but who never missed even one night's sleep. No wonder I kept asking myself why I was not born to be as lucky as them.

A Lucky Escape

When we reached the lakeside, there was a small boat. The van was already there. My father and some fishermen had started to load the boat with our stuff.

We were all wondering if we were going to fit in the boat, but the two fishermen reassured us. They knew how to arrange everything, but our concern was that they were loading it without leaving any space for us to sit.

"Get in the boat!" one of the fishermen said. "It's getting dangerous."

"Where do we sit?" I asked. "The boat is full."

The fisherman who was now looking scared told us to sit on top of our stuff.

"Oh, my Jesus!" I heard my mother crying.

"Look up there in those mountains!" one of the men cried. "People with torches are coming. Hurry up and get in the boat." In all, there was me, my four cousins, my three siblings, my mum, dad and the two fishermen – twelve people in one small fishing boat with all our stuff.

"See?" the fisherman said. "Those are killers. They are coming down here to see if anyone's escaping."

At our place in Kibogora, we were the first people who had fled the country. In the area where we lived, no one else considered doing this. Obviously, the killers thought that we were escaping, or fishermen trying to help Tutsis to escape. We had no idea who had warned them that we were at the lakeside trying to get away.

"Be quick!" the fisherman said. "We have to leave. Maybe someone has told them what we are doing."

One by one we clambered into the boat and found seats.

The two fishermen started the engine.

It sprang into life and we left.

After a few minutes, in the middle of Lake Kivu we heard some gunshots. They were trying to shoot us, but their bullets didn't reach us.

"I told you that the country was in danger and that's why I acted quickly," my father said.

Then, after half an hour, the engine stopped working.

"Oh no!" said one of the fishermen.

We all started panicking, thinking that we were going to drown. I asked my father if we were in any danger, and my father – who also looked scared – told me that he wasn't sure, but that he hoped the fishermen would find a solution.

"I think we have to land at the lakeside and wait for help," one of the fishermen said. "The engine is totally broken, and we can't continue."

We sat at the lakeside, a place with no houses, just the sound of the waves breaking on the shore.

We were as cold as if we had been locked in the freezer. Each of us was shivering. You could hear the teeth chattering. My dad started to make some jokes to make us forget, while the fishermen tried to fix the engine.

"I think this is similar to when you fled from Bujumbura to Zaire in 1972," I said to my father. "You said you went with a small boat, right?"

"Well, not exactly the same. My boat was smaller, with room for only five people. And I was a bit older than you guys."

"Are we going to live at Ijwi Island?" asked my sister.

My father told us that he had a house in Zaire. In 1977, before he went to Rwanda, he built a small house of two bedrooms in a place called Uvira. He had left some people to look after it. We were going to spend a few days in the city of Bukavu before we left for Uvira. Bukavu and Uvira are two cities of Congo located in North Kivu.

"I will first have to go and see if the house is still in good condition," my father said. "It has been more than fifteen years since I saw it."

Hours went by and we were still waiting for the engine to be fixed, while waiting in the darkness at the edge of the lake.

At around 5 a.m., help appeared in the form of some fishermen who brought us a new engine. We continued our journey and at around 7 a.m., we reached the island of Ijwi. We unloaded the boat and left our belongings at the roadside. People were looking at us. Some of them were so poor they had never slept on a mattress or sat on a chair. Seeing these things among our possessions, they tried to rob us.

Once again, I was in a strange country where people used their local language – Gihavu spoken by the Bahavu. The people who live on Ijwi Island are called the Bahavu.

The Miraculous Truck

My father started figuring out how we could get to Bukavu – a journey of three hours from Ijwi Island. We were all hungry and my mother was trying to find us some breakfast from what she had packed. Later, as we ate, we heard a truck coming towards us from behind the hill. We were all nervous.

The vehicle stopped and a man sitting the passenger side of the truck shouted to my father. It was his old childhood friend called Kiba. They lived together when he was in Zaire back in the 1970s.

"Hey Kiba!" my father cried. I will never forget how they hugged. It was as if they had spent 100 years without seeing each other.

"What are you doing here with your family and all this stuff?" Kiba said. "Man, are you still fleeing from all these wars?" Kiba was teasing my father now.

"I swear to God this is really bad, man. I feel terrible for these young children." My father pointed at us sipping tea and munching bread.

"Where are you heading?" Kiba asked.

"We are trying to get to Bukavu."

"Lucky you then," Kiba said. "I'm not leaving you here. Let's start loading your stuff into the back of the truck. It's empty, so there's plenty of room for you and your belongings."

Three hours later we reached Bukavu city.

Poverty and Sickness

We went to live in a very small house at Bagira. The house was built with brown bricks. The floor was simply the dirt of the ground and the roof was made with dry grass. There was no electricity and no water. There was an outside toilet twenty metres from the house.

For my sister, my cousins and I, it wasn't a big issue as we had spent nights sleeping in the bush back in Burundi. But for my two brothers, Lambert and Deo, it was challenging. At first, they refused to enter, saying that those houses were for poor people. My father had to negotiate with them to get them to come inside. What made it worse was the fact that going to the toilet at night was a nightmare in the dark. We had to use a torch. Sometimes the batteries were running low and the light wasn't good.

After three weeks in Bukavu, life was getting tough. My parents couldn't afford to feed eight children without having a job. People now started fleeing from Rwanda to Zaire. Refugee camps had been set up for those who were running away from Rwanda. Some of the refugees started getting dysentery. Children caught chickenpox because of the dirt. Those who had dysentery infected others, even those not in the camps. People died from sickness and hunger. Others, desperate and depressed, chose to kill themselves. Young girls were forced to get married so that they could have at least some chance of surviving.

The citizens of Bukavu were not pleased to see all this sickness and poverty in their country. They became aggressive towards anyone who did not speak Swahili – the local language. It was then that my father thought it would be better for us to move to Uvira as soon as possible. He travelled to Uvira to look at the house he had built in 1977. He figured we should go there before the situation became even worse in Bukavu.

It was time to move again.

My parents and my brothers in Mtabila refugee camp.
My brother Lambert is the one in front of my mother,
and my brother Deo is the one in front of my father.
You can see a part of our house in the camp.
That's the house that we had to build on our own.
(Tanzania – December 1998)

Me and my father in Mtabila refugee camp.
(Tanzania, September 1999)

Me in DR Congo. Despite the hard life and bullies that I was too skinny, I always had a smile on my face. (Uvira, 1995)

Chapter 7
WHERE IS MY HOME?

It was the beginning of July 1994 when we moved to Uvira, a small and lovely city beside Lake Tanganyika. It was very, very, very hot! Sometimes the temperature would even reach 40°C!

The house looked better than the one in Bukavu. There was still no electricity or running water, but at least all ten of us – my parents, my three siblings, my four cousins and I – all fitted in there. In fact, it was like winning the lottery to have our own home. Most of the other refugees lived in camps. Others rented houses and found it difficult to pay their landlords when they couldn't get a job. The rent was higher than normal because people in Zaire thought that refugees were loaded with money hidden in their luggage. Some refugees failed to cope with the hard life in the city and decided to join the refugee camps, where they could at least get free shelter and food.

When we arrived in Uvira, at a place called Kasenga, my father told us that we should all thank God. We had managed to get there safely. The life ahead us was going to be challenging. We were refugees. But we had made it this far. We would make it through the next season of our lives as well.

None of us had a job so the only solution was to work as a team to find some ideas to survive. It was then that my mother decided to start growing vegetables. There was enough space for doing this – there was a big, empty yard.

We went to fetch water from Lake Tanganyika. There was no water around where we lived. Those who had it in their homes would charge us for the water from their taps. But at the lake it was free, and everyone was welcome.

We all knew that we had to get used to this new life. Those of us who were children understood that we needed to be supportive of our parents and show them that together we would conquer every difficulty. So, we all worked as a team. It wasn't going to be easy as a family of ten people unless we believed in collaboration and understanding. My father kept reminding us of his mantra: "Never forget what I told you. When you are a foreigner in a country you must work hard to live. The opportunities will always be there, but priority will be given to citizens of that country. After they have been served, then it will be your turn. This is the way of things."

Finding Home

Even though I had been a foreigner in Rwanda, in Uvira the Congolese constantly reminded me of my status as an alien. To be a refugee in Congo was like a crime. In broad daylight on the streets, people would come up to you and rob or insult you. The local citizens in Uvira were mostly from the Bafulero tribe. The Bafulero spoke their local language – Gifulero – though they also spoke Swahili. There were also some people from another tribe called Bebembe, who lived in Uvira.

Moving around in that area was risky for a foreigner, especially if people heard that you didn't speak any of their local languages. Men used to get robbed – including my father – and girls were often raped.

One day, while others had gone to sleep after our evening prayers, I remained outside sitting with my father under the light of the moon.

"Is there any hope for peace?" I asked him. I knew that we could only go back to Rwanda if there was, otherwise we would have to stay in Uvira.

Before he answered, my father asked me to fetch him a glass of drinking water. It was about 35°C outside.

After he took a sip, he turned to me. "I think there will be no need for us to go back to Rwanda."

He pointed to the far distance.

"See those lights there?"

Millions of lights illuminated the night.

"That is Bujumbura city. So, you see that we are closer to our country than Rwanda. Maybe, when the situation gets better, we can go to Burundi instead of going back to Rwanda."

He paused for a moment, staring at the lights.

"Your home is always the best place," he said.

Then he gestured to the mountains behind us.

"See there, up those mountains? There are people who dream of returning to their homeland, even though they have lived more than 50 years in this country and are considered Congolese. But their roots are in Rwanda."

I was confused so he explained. "That is the Mulenge village and the people who live there are Tutsis descent. They were forced to leave Rwanda years ago because of ethnic conflict. They are called the Banyamulenge.

They will one day go back to Rwanda because it's their country."

I remembered my first and only visit to my country of origin and said, "I don't think I will ever call Burundi my home."

My father was shocked and sad.

"Why?"

I began to cry. "How can I call a place my home when I didn't get the chance to get to know it? I lost my grandparents and I don't even remember their faces. I survived the gunshots, the sickness, the hunger in Burundi, and now I have survived the war in Rwanda. Which place will I call my home?" I was still heartbroken. Then I asked, "How can there ever be unity between two races who keep killing each other and for such a long time? Why, after the colonial period, didn't Hutus and Tutsis live together as one, like they used to?"

"There was too much division and anger," my father replied, "stirred up by those who colonized them. It was so bad that people became like animals."

He sighed and then added, "No one was born with a bad heart, intent on killing others. People have been taught to be like this. In the eyes of God we are all equal; it doesn't matter what ethnic or race you are."

Back to Secondary School

In September 1994, when the school term began in Uvira, my siblings and my cousins who were old enough, started going to school. My cousin Violette and I were in secondary school, and we had to wait for a place before starting.

A few weeks later, my father told us that the council of Uvira, together with some priests who lived there, were planning to open a refugee secondary school as a charity. It didn't take long before the school was opened for young refugee boys and girls (all made of Burundian and Rwandan children). And so, I went back to school. We didn't have to pay for our school fees and the teachers were not paid because it was a charity school.

The teachers were themselves refugees who had been to university or who had teaching experience back in Rwanda or Burundi. My father was one of them. He began teaching History, French and Geography. I was one of his students. There was another Congolese secondary school near our new school called *Institut Mwanga*. To differentiate them, ours was called *Institut Mwanga 2*.

Several months later, my mother also found a job at the primary school my siblings attended, near where we lived in Kasenga.

Even when everyone had things to do, life wasn't easy. My dad wasn't being paid, and my mother struggled to receive a salary from the government. She ended up working as a volunteer too, but she kept going to avoid staying at home doing nothing.

We struggled to get clothes and medicines. Malaria was very common and killed a lot of people. I was the one who was most affected. I used to get sick every month and the only cure for me was injections into both my thighs. I remember some of the medications were beyond their expiry date, but we had no choice. I reached the point where I couldn't walk because of the number of injections. The pills were not strong enough to cure my malaria. I was also so skinny that I was bullied at school. "You have HIV/AIDS," they would say. It's hard to believe that I'm still alive!

An Amazing Answer to Prayer

Our first Christmas in Zaire was celebrated in a simple way and the year that followed was full of struggles. Cash became a critical problem and we could see my parents were doing their best and trying to find a way to feed eight children. They decided to register secretly in the refugee camp so that we could get free food. This wasn't allowed for people living outside the camps. With most of the food, the date had expired but because people were famished, they had no choice but to eat it. For the days when the food was distributed, we had to be at the Kagunga Refugee Camp – a two-hour journey from Uvira city. We were desperate. My mother had decided to grow vegetables and we had never stopped watering them. But suddenly they had stopped growing.

One day, I sent a letter to a childhood friend called Leonie, who had managed to get to Belgium. I always kept in touch with my friends. In the letter, I mentioned that life wasn't that easy for us in Zaire. I didn't get an answer, so I thought maybe she had not received the letter.

One day, my parents didn't come out from their bedroom. They said they were praying. That day we didn't have food in the house; we didn't have breakfast, lunch, nothing. The same afternoon around 3 p.m., I was planning to go and fetch water from Lake Tanganyika. When I left, I saw a car parking beside the road near our house.

A gentleman approached me. He greeted me politely. I greeted him back. I didn't know who he was.

"Are you Kana's daughter?" he asked.

At first, I hesitated to say yes to a stranger.

"Don't be scared," he said. "I am your father's old friend from our childhood. We come from the same village back home in Burundi. We even herded goats together when we were young."

He asked me again if my father was at home but I still hesitated to tell him that my parents were in their bedroom praying.

"Kana, are you there?" the man shouted. "If you are in the house, come out! It's me, your childhood friend Bernard!"

I heard my father opening the door. He was rubbing his eyes as if he thought he was dreaming.

"Oh! Oh! Oh!" both my father and Bernard kept saying while they hugged.

"Oh my God! Kana, is it really you?"

"Oh my God!" my father kept saying back. It had been more than thirty years since they had seen each other. They looked like they were in heaven.

Bernard came and gave a hug to each of us children and then he told my father that he heard that he was in Uvira, through another friend, Bernard's business partner.

Then Bernard called my father to follow him to his car. "Come and help me," he said. "I have got things that I brought for you guys and they need to be lifted by men because they are heavy."

I followed to see what was there.

Food!

Enough food for five months at least.

My father was speechless.

My mother's face was full of joy.

My dad and Bernard finished removing everything from the car, then we sat outside to hear the two men telling stories.

"You know what kids?" Bernard said. "Your father here, he is the one who gave me this life. He always advised me to go to school, have a good education. I sometimes ignored him. You should take his advice and respect him a lot."

I was touched to hear those words. I started to remember how my father always preached the importance of education. If it wasn't for my father's encouragement, I wouldn't have the life I have now.

Later, my mother brought out some food she had cooked from the things that Bernard had brought.

Truly, my parent's prayers had been answered.

Doing Good to Others

That night, after Bernard had left, before we said our bedtime prayers, my father spoke to us all. "Guys! Listen!" He took a deep breath. He was holding back his tears. Eventually, he spoke. "Did you see what happened today?"

We nodded.

"This shows that God exists and that he can answer your prayers. I stayed in the room all day with your mother and we prayed, prayed, prayed, prayed, asking God to show his miracles. We showed God our children, whose mouths we needed to feed, and he showed us his miracles in return – and on the same day! And see what we have now?"

Then he looked at us and asked, "Did I know that Bernard was coming today?"

We shook our heads.

"I did not, but our prayers were answered. So, whenever you get to the point when you think that the world is falling on your head, just put everything in God's hands."

He paused again.

"And another thing, always do good to others and good things will come back to you. Bernard did this because he recognized how important it was for him to go to school. I am telling you, Bernard was a stubborn guy and he never wanted to go to school. I had to push him. Look where he is today. He is now a businessman."

My New Shoe Repair Business

From that time, food wasn't an issue anymore. We still even had a token to get free food from the refugee camp. However, money was needed because most of us children were teenagers – my two cousins Mediatrice and Violette, my sister Annie and my brother Lambert and me. My parents needed cash to take care of us.

One afternoon, my father came home saying that he had a letter for me from Belgium. When I opened it, I saw that it was from Leonie. Inside the envelope she had put some cash. I don't really remember how much it was, but it was in Belgian currency. I immediately gave the money to my father.

"See!" he said, teasing me. "You should write more."

Then he added, "With your generosity, I know you will be successful in life. You are an adventurous girl. I can see it in you."

Days later, I asked my father if I could repair his damaged shoes. He laughed at me, looking at me as if I was crazy.

"Repair my shoes?"

"Yes," I replied. Then I asked my father to get me all the materials I needed for the repairs. I wanted to show him that I could do it. What I liked about my father was that he never doubted that we could do something. He never discouraged us, but instead he gave us a chance to explore and be creative. That same afternoon he brought all the materials and gave me his shoes. I got to work while he sat beside me, watching what I was doing, never uttering a word. He was clearly surprised.

"Where did you learn this?" he asked.

"You remember Ruka who repaired our shoes in Rwanda?" I asked. "I used to sit beside him and watch what he did. I followed every step. That's how I learned to do it. I only needed to practice."

I remember that day my father telling me how proud he was of me. He couldn't believe what he saw me doing (sadly, Ruka was killed during the Rwandan genocide). He then asked everyone at home who had shoes which needed repairing to give them to me.

"We have got free shoe repair, so bring all your shoes!"

From that time, I started repairing everyone's shoes at home, which saved us the money we would have paid someone else to do it. Where we lived in Africa, you didn't have to take certain types of shoes to the big shoe repair place. We wore simple shoes. I couldn't fix a heel, but I could fix other problems with normal shoes.

A Family of Entrepreneurs

As the days went by, my sister Annie, my brother Lambert, and my cousin Mediatrice, asked my father to give them a small amount of cash to start a small business. They told him they wanted to sell salted peanuts and bubble gum.

My father hesitated to let Annie, Lambert and Mediatrice go into business because he was worried they might forget about school. But they promised they would keep doing great at school, and that they would run their business after school. What touched my father was when they told him that they saw how hard it was to feed eight children, and that they wanted to help him. My father almost cried.

Finally, he gave each of them small amount of money – five USA dollars each, which was then a lot of money in Zaire.

The three of them started selling salted peanuts and bubble gum and their business seemed to be growing. My father appreciated this, as the cash contributed a lot towards our lifestyle in Uvira. We were really a very good team – a family trying to help each other.

Life seemed to be going well. We had adopted a simple life and our only real battle was to get the medicine for malaria, which was a common sickness.

The Terrible Teens

I was 15 years old and I was becoming interested in teenage things. I liked going to school, but I also liked hanging around with my teenage friends. I had my two best friends Liliane and Alice and our only leisure pursuit was the Scouts activities. My father gave me permission to go to these, but my mother was a bit more cautious and strict. Since I had already started my monthly periods, she was worried and one day, after my father came home from work, I heard her saying something to him:

"What if she gets pregnant?"

The reason she asked this was because I would be meeting boys during the Scouts activities. She didn't realize that I was listening in on their conversation.

Most of the time my father came home late in the evening when everybody was sleeping. And every time he got inside the house, he would gently call my name. I would wake up and give him food, which I enjoyed doing because when he sat eating, I would sit beside him and have a chat with him.

That evening he did the same thing and we sat outside.

Then my father started to speak. "You know us man, we are clever."

I always liked the way he said 'us man' referring to 'us men'. I thought that was cool.

"Us man can be clever at getting into girls," he said. "Girls are vulnerable. So, be clever and more intelligent than them."

He paused and then added, "You know, when a young girl gets pregnant at a young age, her life will be finished. Her future is zero."

I listened carefully without saying a word. I knew my parents were worried about me because at that time HIV/AIDS was common and a lot of young girls were affected. Most of these girls were desperate because of their poverty. They would sell themselves and sleep with rich men for money. But I logged every word that my father had told me when advising me to be careful with boys. That advice helped me. I always remembered that the most important thing was to concentrate on putting my education first.

The Dangers of Being Tall and Thin

During July 1996, Uvira wasn't as safe as we had thought. We could see more soldiers and police in the city, sometimes even on the streets. We were ordered to be in our houses by 7 p.m. We didn't know what was going on but there were rumours that they suspected an attack from the mountains where the Banyamulenge lived.

One day in August, my father was due to go to the city centre to exchange some dollars into the local currency called Nouveau Zaire. My mother asked him if we could go together so that I could buy some dried fish for dinner. When we reached the Bridge of Mulongwe, two policemen shouted at my father.

"Munyamulenge uyo mukamate!" This is Swahili and means, 'That's a Munyamulenge! Arrest him!' The two policemen handcuffed my father.

"I am not a Munyamulenge! I am a Burundian refugee!" my father insisted.

I was scared to see my father being handcuffed. I didn't know what to do.

"Murundi gani mulefu hiyo kama Banyamulenge!" ('How can you say that you are a Burundian as tall as you are, like Banyamulenge people?') they shouted.

At this time, they were arresting anyone they suspected of being a Munyamulenge. Most of these were being identified by their physical appearance – by whether they were tall and thin – and because of the bad conditions in Uvira, my father had become very lean.

The policemen searched my father's pockets and the first thing they found were the dollars he was going to exchange.

My father told me to go quickly and tell my mum that they had arrested him.

When I got home, instead of telling my mother what had happened, I started crying.

"What's wrong? What's wrong?" my mother asked, together with my cousins and siblings. Finally, I managed to tell them that my father had been arrested.

Without delay, my mother went to see Noki, who was well-known in Uvira as a leading member of Mobutu's party, the 'Popular movement of the Revolution'. She asked him if he could help us get my father out of police custody. He was from the Babembe tribe and was the husband of my mother's cousin.

Later in the evening, my mother came back saying that my father was in a prison called Mbwa Mabe. Two days later, my father was released. When he came home, he told us there were a lot of Banyamulenge being tortured in that prison. Apparently, there had been some killing going on between the Babembe tribe and the Banyamulenge. In the area of Uvira, many of the Banyamulenge had been attacked and arrested, and many of these were tortured and killed in prison. Since there were rumours that the Banyamulenge were going to be attacking soon, the police had started arresting everyone they thought was a Munyamulenge, including my father.

Another Deportation

A month later, in September 1996, the government ordered the military to deport all foreigners in the country, and that included refugees. Everyone was panicking; we knew that Congolese would carry out the orders of the government.

One day, my mother, my cousins Violette and Mediatrice, and I went to the camp to get food. The next morning, when we had planned to return home to Uvira, we saw a lot of soldiers surround the camp. Some were well-armed. Others were standing on top of their military trucks. They were forcing refugees to get into the trucks to be deported to their countries. We were asked what our country was and allocated a truck heading back to Rwanda. I tried to run but was chased by a soldier who beat me with his gun, forcing me to get into the truck. He asked me which country I came from, and I told him Burundi. So, I was put in the truck which was deporting Burundians. I didn't know where my mother, my cousins Violette and Mediatrice were. We were all scattered.

Inside the trucks, everyone was crying – men, women, and children. I cried and cried. I was suffering from terrible back pain because of the violence I had suffered at the hands of the soldier. The vehicle started and before long we were at the border of Burundi and Congo, at a place called Katumba. Burundi soldiers were waiting to receive those being deported. The last time I had been in Burundi was during the war in 1993. That time I had gone there of my own free will. This time I was being deported without knowing what was going on. I wept so many tears that day. I will never forget it.

The soldiers took us to some tents in a ready-made campsite in Katumba and they gave me a place with people that I didn't know. They gave me two blankets, one to sleep on and the other one to cover myself. I couldn't sleep. I was crying all night.

The next day, the military came to register our details. When I revealed my name and the place where

I was born, one of the guards said, "They have brought us a Rwandan instead of a Burundian." I felt rejected because of my place of birth and my language – rejected by the people who I thought would surely recognize I was really a Burundian. Then another soldier said, "We should take you to Rwanda." I was in shock. How had I been deported to a country I had never lived in, even though it was meant to be my country of origin? It was simply terrible.

A day later, I saw my mother and my cousins, Violette and Mediatrice. They had been brought in a different truck, and they had spent the night in a different tent. When I saw them, I was relieved and stopped crying.

However, my father was in Uvira and he didn't know what had happened to us. When I took a walk to the road with my mother and my cousins, my mother saw a car which was going to Uvira and she asked the driver if he could inform my father that we had been deported to Burundi.

After five days in Katumba, my father found someone to help us escape the camp and go back to Uvira. By that time, the security in Burundi had deteriorated. On our way back to Uvira, we went through the bush and crossed the river Rusizi at midnight.

A lot of refugees were deported by force to their countries, including the Banyamulenge who were born and lived all their years in Congo. They were deported to Rwanda, a country they had never lived in.

Mai Mai and Magic Water

On our return, we found that the security in Uvira remained critical. We even started hearing some gunshots. During that time, all boys aged 15 and older were ordered to join a militia group called the Mai Mai, meaning 'Water Water'. This group believed in witchcraft. They were brainwashed to believe that if they drank what they called 'magical water', bullets wouldn't kill them. These people would knock on each door to recruit boys and men to join the militia group.

One day they came to our door.

"I will not get involved in any fighting or killing," my father told them. "I am a Burundian not a Congolese!"

This was the same answer he had given the Interahamwe in Rwanda during the genocide. The terrible thing is that a lot of people who joined this Mai Mai militia group died, whilst believing that their magic would protect them. They had been told that if they were struck by a bullet, water would flow from their bodies, not blood.

One night in the first week of October, we heard some gunshots and we all went outside to see what was happening. We had a visitor at the time, a friend of my father named Leon, but known as Manwangali. My father and Leon went outside to see what was going on. The rest of us he told to stay inside.

I shook my head, saying to myself, "No! No! No! Not war again!" Uvira had become my home. I felt comfortable there and now this!

My father, and Leon came back inside, and they told us not to worry, that the gunshots were far up in the mountains. We all went to bed peacefully.

On the morning of the 15 October, we woke up and had breakfast. After breakfast, my father and Leon went to visit their friend several houses away from our home. Around 12 p.m., we heard continuous shooting.

"Oh my God! Not again!" I sighed. It was war.

Luckily enough, everyone was at home. About five minutes later, my father came running back. "Pack what is necessary. We have to leave right now," he said. He was confused; he didn't understand what was happening, and this made us panic. "Get the food, two cooking pots, a bit of cooking oil, but don't pack any clothes. Wear as many clothes as you can on your body. Be quick we have to go." Where? I didn't know. Everyone was scared now. All we could hear was gunshots.

While the rest of us panicked, my mother packed her clothes and photo albums into a very big suitcase as the shooting got louder in the mountains.

We had a blue tent which my father asked me to take, saying we were going to need to use it for sleeping. It was a plain tent of four-by-five metres.

Each child was given a small bag of food. My dad filled a briefcase with documents and diplomas. I thank God that my mother filled her suitcase with her photos. Today, I still have my childhood pictures.

"I won't help you with that big suitcase," my father told my mother.

"It's okay. I will carry it. Don't worry," my mother replied.

We locked the door and left with Leon.

Underneath the Mango Tree

We walked about 6 kilometres before joining a crowd of hundreds of people fleeing to the south.

"Stay together guys!" my father shouted.

The crowd kept growing and every time we approached a village, more people from that village joined until it became a million people fleeing. The more we walked, the more the sound of gunfire got heavier and heavier. You could hear people crying, both men and women, saying in Swahili, "Banyarwanda banatumaliza mungu weee!" meaning 'Rwandan people are finishing us, oh Lord!'

You could hear people calling out, "Mama! Papa! Auntie! Uncle!" Different names were being shouted. Mothers were calling their children. Children who were lost were calling their parents, uncles or aunties. It was so sad.

Everyone looked hopeless and no one knew where we were heading. Leon said that we should go to his place in South Kivu – Baraka.

No one looked behind. There was simply no time to see if you were still with your family. All you could see anyway was the luggage on peoples' heads. The only way to know if you were still with your family was by shouting out their names.

We walked kilometres and kilometres, under the sun in temperatures of 40°C, with no sign of water. We couldn't stop and take a rest because we were scared of being killed. From time to time, someone fainted, fell, and died. You just had to keep walking. There was no alternative.

After walking for five hours non-stop, it was already dark. At 6 p.m., my father shouted all our names to let us know that we were going to stop and get a rest. By that time the shooting had calmed so we left the crowd of people and went to the roadside under a big mango tree. We were all thirsty but there was no water.

Other people also took a rest just under that same mango tree. I asked them where they had found the water that they were drinking. This guy showed me a river which was just a few meters away. Thank God that river was not far. I couldn't imagine walking again.

We fetched some wood for the fire to cook, as well as some water from the river. While we ate, we watched people walking by. There were women with children on their backs, men with luggage on their heads, children looking tired and confused, everyone walking with hopeless faces.

And that's how our faces looked too.

We set up the blue tent and sat in it and ate.

"See guys," my father said. "I told you to pack the important things. FOOD! Not like your mother here, who only packed her clothes." He was playing with us. Later, after we had eaten, we all slept in the tent. It wasn't a proper sleep – just enough to give our bodies a rest before we continued walking.

Never go Back!

It was the season for mangoes and the all way we ate mangoes from the trees. We would stop to go and drink water at a river – water which wasn't clean, sometimes because of animal waste. This was my worst experience fleeing a country.

One day at the end of 1996, we went down to the river. As I bent down to put my hands in the water, I saw a severed hand surrounded by blood. It was followed in the current by a severed, braided, woman's head. I screamed. They were killing people up in the mountains and then cutting their bodies into pieces and throwing the body parts into the river. I still can't forget what I saw. Even though I have tried to forget it, the images still come back, like uninvited guests.

A few days later, Leon said that we were about to get to a place called Mboko. From there we could get a small fishing boat to Baraka, his place. We all thought it would be safer to stay there.

At about 1 p.m., we heard gunshots again. The bullets were spraying everywhere. The gunfire was so loud. We knew enough to realize that it was coming from behind us, up in the mountains, and in front of us, where we were heading. I wanted to run back.

"Never in your life go back, especially during a war!" my father shouted.

Everyone ran.

This time it was terrible.

We lost each other. My four cousins, my brother Lambert, and Leon, were all scattered and missing. I remained with my father, my sister Annie, my mother, and my brother Deo.

We all ran down to Lake Tanganyika, where we thought it would be safe.

People were being struck down by bullets. You could see someone in front of you falling and dying straight away. Others were shaking their necks where they lay, their hands growing limp, their legs struggling against death. Children were sucking their dead mothers' breasts. There was nothing you could do to help. You just jumped over them and continued running for dear life. They, meanwhile, would give in to death after a while. No one was there to save them or bury them. It was terrible.

We continued to run to the lake, thinking that if we ran to the water, maybe we could find a fishing boat to rescue us. But we were wrong. When we got closer, we saw people being killed ahead of us. The lake was full of blood. Everywhere, boats were being riddled with holes from the guns and were sinking in the water. By then, I didn't know that those who were doing the killing were just a few metres behind us. I was still with my parents, my sister Annie, and my brother Deo at this point.

Running from War

When we entered the lake, I heard men shouting, telling us to come out from the water. When I looked behind, there were four men fully armed in kaki. I knew then that was the last day of my life.

"Lie down now!" the men shouted.

Myself, my father, my mother, my sister Annie and my young brother Deo (4 years old at the time) lay down on the sand, with our legs in the water.

"What were you doing in the water?" The four men were standing just in front of us now, pointing guns into our faces.

"We were trying to escape," my mother said.

My father kept quiet because he knew that it was the end. Men were being killed without pity.

"We are running because of the war," I said.

"Where have you come from?"

"The Babembe area," I replied. That was a lie. I was in a state of panic.

"Where in Babembe do you come from?" one of them asked.

"Swima," I said, lying again. Swima was a place we had left before we reached Mboko, where the shooting begun.

"She is lying. They are not Babembe," one of the killers said.

"Don't kill them! They are not Babembe!" another one said. The entire conversation was in Swahili.

"Come out from the water and go get dry, then stay in your houses," the men said.

When we stood up, one of them said to his friends, "Kill those two men. They are Babembe." They had seen two men trying to escape. They shouted at them to stop but they kept on running. One of the killers shot them dead. When they fired, we thought they had shot us, so close was the sound of the guns.

We all stood up and walked without knowing where we were going. The first house we saw open, that's where we entered. In that house there was the dead body of someone they had just shot. The family was waiting for the shooting to stop so they could bury it.

We all sat in the same corner. No one talked. We were desperate. My father was wondering how he was going to explain to his brother that all his children were missing. I was wondering why those men didn't kill us when they had the chance, why they didn't shoot my father when men were being hunted down and killed. I was also wondering why they had asked us where we lived and if we knew the reason why we were fleeing. I didn't know the answer until nineteen years later, when I read the book *Not My Worst Day* by Alex Mvuka Ntung.

In his book, the author explained more about the war in Congo, especially in the area of Uvira which we were fleeing from. He described how the Banyamulenge were fighting to protect their people who had suffered from the injustice of being mistreated by the Babembe tribe for many years. This made me remember how they had arrested my father, thinking wrongly that he was a Munyamulenge, and how in prison the Banyamulenge were being tortured by the Babembe tribe. Then I remembered how the four men had recognized that I was lying when I said we were from the Babembe area and had decided not to kill us but instead let us go.

Looking for the Missing Ones

After the shootings had cooled down in Mboko, my mother decided to go and check every dead body to see if any of my cousins or my brother had been killed. She looked at every young face, because my cousins and my brother were all young. After two hours, my mum came back looking desperate. She hadn't found them.

We spent days in Mboko in a house vacated by fugitives. People were still fleeing. Others were coming out from hiding in the bush and continued to walk. We went and stood at the roadside to see if my cousins or my brother were passing by. We saw people we knew and asked them, but no one could help.

We gave up and decided to continue fleeing. Where? We had no idea. When we left Uvira, Leon had said that we were going to his place in Baraka, but Leon was now missing too.

The day before we decided to continue our flight from the country, my mother woke up early in the morning and said that she was going to try one last time to go and stand by the road and see if she could find my cousins or my brother.

An hour later, she came back with my brother.

I ran quickly into the house where we were hiding to tell my father that my brother was found. My father asked my mother how she found him.

"I was just in the middle of the road walking, and I saw many metres away one young boy who looked lost and lonely, I kept walking. The boy walked towards me and, when I looked, well, it was Lambert."

Then my father asked my brother what happened when the shootings began.

"When we all ran, I missed you guys and I followed Leon. And when we got down to the lake, they shot at us and we hid in the long grass by the lakeside with Leon."

My brother went on to say that Leon was hiding at a place near where my mother had found him.

My father thanked God, but he was still not satisfied. He had his four children with him, but his brother's children were still missing. He really looked desperate, his tears rolling down his cheeks.

That afternoon, my brother went to show my father where he and Leon had been hiding. They found Leon and thirty minutes later, my father, Leon and my brother Lambert came back saying that we had to leave as soon as possible. People were saying that the place where we hid in Mboko was going to be under attack again.

In the evening, around 6 p.m., we made our way between some palm fields. I had no idea where we were going. Leon had told us before that we needed to head to a place where we could find a boat to take us to Tanzania. We walked hours at night in the palm field. It was very dark and scary. All I could hear was the sound of frogs. We were lucky that the moon in the sky was lighting our way.

Four hours later, we reached Kenya Kangeta. The place was deserted. There had been a terrible attack; houses were destroyed, others were left open by those fleeing. The only people present were dead, and you could not even see a bird flying there.

When I heard Leon saying that we had reached Kenya Kangeta, I was surprised. "Wait a minute, did you just say Kenya?" I asked.

He replied, "Not Kenya the country. The person who gave this place that name came from Kenya."

The rain started falling now. We opened our tent, sat on the grass and sheltered until the rain stopped. I had a terrible belly pain and was worried that I was going to have my period. I had no sanitary products or even an extra cloth to use. Thank God it wasn't what I was thinking. The two months we were fleeing, everything switched off and I don't remember having any periods at all. A miracle!

My Mother was Right After All!

When we woke up, Leon said, "We're going to Lake Tanganyika to see if we can find any fishermen with a small boat to take us to the island called Ubwali. There, we can get a big boat to Tanzania."

When we got at the lake, we couldn't find anyone to help us. We could see the island in front of us, but how to get there?

There was one unfinished house near the lake; a house with no windows or doors. We spent almost a week in that house. People had left potatoes, tomatoes, sweet potatoes, and that's what we ate. Free food. All we did was fetch wood for the fire. We used water from the lake and we all slept in our tent.

One afternoon, Leon and my father decided to try and find someone who could help us to reach Ubwali. They returned to tell us we were leaving that night. We used a small fishing boat to get to the island, which took us all night. In the middle of Lake Tanganyika, water started getting inside the boat. It wasn't a boat with an engine; it was a small rowing boat. Some of us started removing the water from the boat to avoid it sinking while others paddled, but the water kept coming into the boat. We prayed, prayed, and prayed. Everyone helped to paddle. We could see the island in front of us. Finally, we managed to beach the boat on the shore.

There we found a lot of people we knew, who also lived in Uvira. Most of them were stuck on the island because they couldn't find a way to leave and escape to Tanzania. To do that, people needed cash. But where to find cash? There was none.

My mother came up with an idea to sell a few of her clothes to the people who said they could help us to get to Tanzania. They were all good quality so, in the end, the suitcase that we teased mother for carrying saved us.

After we sold my mother's clothes, we paid the fishermen to take us to Tanzania and that same night we left Ubwali Island. We spent all night on Lake Tanganyika, almost forty people in one medium-sized fishing boat.

Me, after finding out that I was pregnant with my
daughter. This day, everything was confusing to me.
I didn't see clearly what my future was like.
(Cape Town, July 2000)

My brother Lambert, me in the middle and my sister
Annie, in Maputo - Mozambique. My siblings and I always
laugh when we see how we posed for this picture.
We thought that was cool. (May 2000)

Me, the very first day I arrived in Cape Town. I was on
the public phone talking to my siblings who were in
Mozambique. I was telling them that I love Cape Town,
that they will be joining me soon and start a new
life in South Africa. (June 2000)

Chapter 8
SOMETHING'S NOT RIGHT

The morning of 10 January 1997, we reached Tanzania. We had disembarked at the side of the lake and we didn't know where to go or what to do next. We had spent a sleepless night on the lake, so we looked for somewhere on the shore where we could pitch our tent and rest. Our minds, accustomed to war, now needed to become used to peace.

I have never seen people who care about the security of their country like the Tanzanians. Everyone in Tanzania behaves as if they were in the police, from children to adults. Consequently, Tanzania has been one of the most peaceful countries in all Africa. When we pitched our tent, there were no adults nearby, only children playing and swimming in the lake without a care in the world.

After about forty-five minutes, when we had made ourselves comfortable and tried to snatch some sleep, we saw four policemen approaching our tent. It must have been the children who told them we were there.

"Habari Zenu?" they greeted us in Swahili. ('How are you doing?')

They were very calm, with no hint of aggression, but because of the trauma of all the killings in Zaire, we reacted nervously.

"Don't panic," one of the policemen said. "We are here to help you. This is Tanzania where we have peace and you are safe. This area is called Kigoma." Kigoma is one of the cities in the west of the country.

"Munawongea luga gani?" the other policeman asked in Swahili. ('What language do you speak?')

I knew from my history lessons that the citizens of Tanzania spoke Swahili, but their Swahili sounded different from the one I had learned in Zaire. I liked their accent though. Tanzanian Swahili is the proper Swahili. It is the Swahili that people speak worldwide. Fortunately, I was able to learn the official Swahili language.

The police registered our details and one of them then used his walkie-talkie radio to report to headquarters that they had found some refugees down at the lake. Later, we saw a police van parking near us. The police asked us to come with them. "We're driving you to a refugee camp," they said.

Tanzania had a lot of refugee camps dotted around the country. There were camps for Rwandans who fled their country in 1959 and 1994; camps for Burundians who fled in 1972 and 1993, and they were now creating more camps for those fleeing in 1996 from Zaire. We were told that they were taking us to one of the new camps called Mtabila Refugee Camp at Kasulu, about 200 kilometres from Kigoma.

We waited with many other refugees. As we stood there, we kept looking at the new refugees to see if we could find any of my cousins. None of them showed up and we began to fear they had been killed.

Late in the afternoon, we were put in a very big truck with about sixty people on board. We sat like sheep as we headed to Mtabila Refugee Camp in Kasulu. I don't remember how long it took for us to get there, but we arrived around 7 p.m. The truck had driven slowly because the road wasn't all paved, and it was raining heavily.

The camp was in the bush, and by that, I mean a forest.

"Oh my God, where da hell is this place?" I cried, my eyes wide open.

There were other refugees who had been there for about three years and they seemed to have grown used to living in the forest. That night, they offered us some blankets, tents and drinking cups, and they directed us to a big hall full of other refugees where we had to sleep until we registered the next day.

The next day, when we registered we were given tokens for getting our food. We were offered more blankets, cooking pots, eating plates, petrol lamps and a plot of land where we had to build our house.

"What da hell is this forest and what da hell are we doing here?" I asked myself again. Maybe this was my destination and my destiny. Maybe this was how I was going to spend the rest of my life – as a forest-dweller.

Facing Off with a Monster

We cut some trees in the forest so that we could use the wood to build our house. The tents they had given us were to be used for the roof, doors, and windows. We could cut the canvas to cover the openings. We were given everything we needed to do the job, including hammers, machetes, and nails.

When we went up to the hill to cut some trees, my father tried to put a smile on our faces. But it wasn't so easy. The forest was full of nasty surprises.

"Don't move!" my father suddenly said.

"Stay calm!" he whispered again.

We all froze! It was a snake! And I had never seen such a long and ugly snake in my entire life. Never, never, never!

We kept looking at the snake which was now a few metres from us. There were seven of us – my dad, my mum, my three siblings, myself, and Leon. I didn't know where that creature was going, but it looked hungry and was searching for food. Fortunately, it kept moving, continuing on its hunt.

We now started cutting wood from the trees in earnest, my father telling funny stories to help distract us. When we had finished, we carried the wood on our heads and walked back down to the camp. We did this for about three days before we started building our house, having created a plan of how we wanted our home to look.

We used the tents and some dried grass to create the roof. The doors and windows we covered using canvas from the tents.

With that done, we started our new lives in the refugee camp.

A Miraculous Reunion

In the camp, there were two days each month designated for food distribution. The food was mostly corn maize flour, dry peas, dry beans, cooking oil, and sea salt. As the days went by we started growing our own potatoes, sweet potatoes, tomatoes, carrots, and cassava in the back yard.

In the camp, the Tanzanians had set up a local market where they sold other things, like clothes and kitchen implements. Some of the people struggled to get the money to buy extra household items brought by the Tanzania citizens who lived outside the camp. Different fruits were sold in the market, but few people could afford them.

In the camp, we learned to accept the life we were living. There were a lot of snakes and sometimes we went to sleep afraid of what they might do to us in the night.

Every time new refugees arrived, we would go and see if any of our cousins were among them. One day, when we watched new arrivals jumping from the trucks, we had the most wonderful surprise. We saw my cousin Mediatrice. It was a miracle! We hugged and hugged her, weeping tears of joy. She had come with a family who had found her crying on the road after she went missing during the gunfire in Mboko. My father went to say thank you to them for saving my cousin's life.

A month later, just as unexpectedly, another truck drove in with new refugees and who should be among them this time but my other cousins, Violette, Perfect, and Willene. That day was a joyful and crazy one. We all sat outside that night sharing what had happened when each of us ran from the gunfire in Mboko, how each of us had thought that the others who went missing had died. We felt like the luckiest people on earth.

My father sent a letter to my uncle telling him that all his children had been found alive. My uncle Sophonie was also living in a refugee camp called Kanembwa in Kibondo district. No more than two months later, he came to take my cousins to go and join him and their other siblings who had remained with their dad. My cousin Violette now lives in Australia. My uncle

Sophonie and the rest of his seven children are in Canada.

The Visitor from Lusaka

After three months living in Mtabila camp, we started going to school. We had no classrooms, so we sat under the trees for our lessons. When it rained we would stop and go back to our house. This was how I lived my life, and this is how I expected things to remain – living in the forest. But I was wrong.

Six months later, at the end of June, I was busy cooking before I could go for my Scouts activities when I saw Patrick, one of my friends, walking towards me with another tall guy. Patrick greeted me with a kiss on both cheeks, and the other guy introduced himself. "My name is Chris and I am from Zambia," he said.

"Hi, I am Josée. Nice to meet you."

I offered both Chris and Patrick a seat, but Patrick had to leave for some other business. I had never met Chris and I was keen to hear his story. He didn't look like someone who had lived in the camps, though. He didn't have the telltale signs of poor nutrition and vitamin deficiency.

Chris asked if my father was around, but I told him that he wouldn't be home until late in the evening. We were taught to respect visitors, so I made him feel comfortable. Later, my father returned. I told him that we had a visitor from Lusaka, which is where Chris told me he was from. My father greeted him warmly.

Chris told my father that he had a letter for him sent by a man named Adam. His big brother had married my mother's cousin, so he was a family friend. Adam had left the camp to go and live in Zambia, which is where he had met Chris. Chris reached into his backpack, and he handed an envelope to my father.

"This is the letter," he said.

My father opened it, read it, read it again, then again and again. He asked Chris how life was in Lusaka. He was interested in learning everything he could. Meanwhile, I started asking myself why my father was so interested in Lusaka. During the conversation, Chris told my father that he was going to Germany in four months and that he had a scholarship to go and study there.

The next day, my father called me and my sister. He said that he wanted to go with 'his girls' for a walk. He always used to tease my mother, telling her, "me with my girls and you with your boys."

As we walked together, my father popped a question. "What would you say if I decided to send you somewhere for a good education?"

"What do you mean?" I asked.

My father held us both. "Look, the letter Chris gave me yesterday was Adam asking if I should send both of you to go and study in Zambia."

"Zambia? Annie and me?" I gasped. "What about you guys?"

My father wiped his face with his big hand and his long fingers. "If you don't want to go, I won't force you. But let me ask you something. Do you like living in this forest? Do you want to continue having your lessons sitting under the trees? Do you know that there are other children who can't get the chance you're being offered for a good education? Even here in the camps, there are many people who want that opportunity, but they can't find someone to give it to them."

"Are we going alone?" my sister asked.

"Chris will go with you both."

It was clear now that my father wanted me to go to Zambia. Adam had sent my ticket with Chris. My father was going to find someone to lend him some money for my sister's ticket so that we could go together.

My sister and I were now worried, but my father kept looking at me and my sister, waiting to hear our decision.

"I'm scared that I won't see you all again," I said. I told him I was frightened that war might break out again and that I might lose my family forever this time. I really didn't know what to say.

"I understand that you are scared and still traumatized from what you have experienced," my father said, "but Zambia is a peaceful country like Tanzania. Trust me as a history man, I know what I am talking about. Don't you know that during apartheid in South Africa, most South Africans fled to Zambia?" Then he added, "It's okay. We will join you there too."

"Okay, I am cool with that," I said.

"Me too," my sister said.

My father gave us a warm hug. During the rest of the walk, he advised us to be careful with boys, and to make our education the highest priority.

"Be good girls for Adam and his wife and appreciate them for letting you go and live in their home in Lusaka," he concluded.

Suspicious Minds

The next day, Chris asked me if I could show him around the camp. As we went, I told him that my father said that we were going back with him to Lusaka.

"Yeah, actually Adam told me," Chris said. "And there is a chance that you could go to Germany too," he added.

Why Germany? Why Europe? I thought.

As we walked, we passed my friend Nella's house, and I told her that I was soon leaving the camp to go to Lusaka.

As my tour of the camp finished, Chris asked me what my religion was.

"I am a Christian and belong to the Free Methodist Church," I answered.

"I'm a Roman Catholic," he said, "which is what you will be too."

I had no idea what he meant by that. Why would I need to change my religion if I went to Zambia? Something was not right. I could feel it.

When we got home, my father told me that he had found someone to lend him the $100 for my sister's ticket. Before we left the camp, my father gave us the briefcase he had bought in Switzerland in 1993 when he went on his work mission. My father had carried that briefcase all the way from Rwanda to Tanzania, and he always used to carry his important documents.

"If anything happens," he said, "You can always sell it. It's a very classic diplomatic briefcase."

We never did sell it.

We still have that briefcase to this day.

I was 17 years old, my sister was 15, but my father gave me the responsibility to look after my sister. Then he said, "Jo, you know you are older than your sister. Take care of her. Even though you are still young yourself, I trust you."

My father begged us to be good girls and make him proud.

"I believe in you," he said.

Something Isn't Right Here

On 20 June 1997, four days after Chris had arrived, we secretly left the camp to avoid being seen by the security guards, and we headed to Kigoma city to get our travel documents. We spent five days in Kigoma before these were released to us. These were the only documents that would work for us, and to get them we had to give money to corrupt officials in immigration.

I still suspected that something was not quite right, that something about this whole trip was being hidden from us. This came to a head when Chris told me that my sister had to go back to the camp because the man arranging our travel documents had asked him for too much money.

"If my sister has to go back to the camp," I said, "then I am going back with her!"

"No!" Chris snapped.

"Why not?" I asked.

"Adam needs you more than your sister. And anyway, it's better for you to go and study in Zambia because you're older. Your sister can come later."

I stared into the air, trying to figure out what was going on, why his reactions were so weird, why I was needed more than my sister.

"I am not going with you if my sister has to go back to the camp," I repeated. "I will go with her."

Chris didn't say a word until the next morning when he told me that he had also found my sister's travel documents. He didn't look pleased at all.

On 25 June, we took the boat from Kigoma. This time it was huge compared to the small fishing boat we used before.

We spent three days on Lake Tanganyika before we could get to the border of Zambia at the Port of Mpulungu. My sister and I enjoyed our time on the boat to the full, watching small boats with men fishing, going downstairs to the restaurant, having a really good time. But all the while I kept asking myself why Chris was unhappy. He had a weird look and he didn't speak to us that much.

I knew something was hidden behind that, but I didn't find out the truth until I heard it from Chris' lips.

Me and Gilbert. Little did we know that one day
this picture will be in the book that he inspired me
to write. Thank you G.

Chapter 9
A DERANGED MARRIAGE

On the morning of 28 June, after three days in the boat, we reached the port of Mpulungu. We walked to the immigration office and handed over our travel documents which said that we were Tanzanians. The officers looked at us, then talked to us, trying to check if we knew how to speak Swahili. They asked us where we lived in Tanzania and what we had come to do in Zambia. We told them that we lived in Kigoma and that we were going on a holiday in Lusaka. They stamped our travel documents and we passed through a large gate into Zambian territory.

The first thing we did was have breakfast in a restaurant. Everywhere people were either speaking in English or in the local language in Mpulungu. Not for the first time, I felt like a foreigner in a strange land. No one was speaking in French or Swahili. I didn't know how to speak English. I prayed that no one would talk to me.

As we sat in the restaurant after our meal, Chris asked me if we could chat outside. We sat on a bench in the sunshine.

"I need to tell you the whole story," he said, looking serious. "I went to ask Adam if he knew a girl I could marry before I go to Germany because I didn't want to marry a Zambian. I wanted someone from my country with my background and culture. Adam told me that he knew a girl in the refugee camp in Tanzania and that girl was you. He said that the easy way to get you to Lusaka was to tell your father that you were coming to study in Zambia. So, that's why Adam wrote his letter."

I felt as if I was about to faint.

I recovered but I didn't talk for several minutes. The truth was out now. Somehow, I managed to hold back my tears. I felt very, very, very sad – sad to hear that someone my father trusted as a friend and as family could lie to him, sad that I was being manipulated into getting married at such a young age. Adam had remembered the thing that my father prized most – putting education first – and had used this to persuade him to let his two daughters go with Chris to Lusaka.

"I am only 17, for God's sake," I said to Chris. "I'm not getting married this young. I don't even know you. And if I did, you wouldn't be the kind of guy I would date anyway."

Chris wasn't a bad-looking man; he was cool and even handsome, but I wasn't into dating someone. I had gone through a lot, cutting short my studies because my life had been in danger. What I really wanted was to go back to school, achieve my goals and make my father proud. My father was my inspiration. I tried to imagine his face when he heard that I had been married and left for Germany.

"If I want to go to Europe," I told Chris, "I'll go because I want to go there, not because I'm married to you."

Chris started begging me. "I'll give you everything you've ever wanted, if only you agree to be my girlfriend."

"Hell no, and hell to the no!" I said.

"Do you want me to go back to your parents and pay the dowry?" he asked.

"You didn't hear what I said," I shouted. "You don't even have a tiny chance." And with that, I walked back into the restaurant and straight to the bathroom where I looked at myself in the mirror. There were tears pouring from my eyes. I washed my face and hurried back to my sister.

"It's okay," Chris said. "I will leave it to Adam when we get to Lusaka."

"What's going on?" my sister asked.

"It's a long story sis," I said. "I'll tell you later."

One Lie after Another

A little later, we took the coach to Kasama where we had to connect with the train to Lusaka. It was my first time in a train and I felt like I was on the other side of the world – from East to Southern Africa.

We arrived at Lusaka around 7 p.m. and went straight to Adam's place. Adam and his wife looked excited to see us; they hugged us and welcomed us to their home. I pretended to look happy, but I was angry and hurt.

Chris was the one who had secured this accommodation for Adam, his wife, and his daughter. He had even helped them to start a grocery shop. I guess they wanted to pay Chris back for all that he'd done, and the payback was to get me to marry Chris.

That night, I waited to see if Adam would mention anything, but he didn't say a word about the plan.

The next day, Adam's wife asked me if Chris had told me anything. I told her that I was hurt to hear about the proposed marriage and I felt so disappointed at the way they had manipulated my father.

"Don't be stupid Jo," she said. "Remember, this guy's planning to go to Europe and that will be your chance too."

I looked into her eyes and told her that I wasn't going to date Chris even if he was planning to go to Europe.

"We'll discuss this when Adam gets home from work," she said.

Late in the evening, after we had finished dinner, Adam and his wife called me. We sat in their bedroom and they started trying to convince me to date Chris. I asked them if they remembered how old I was, and asked them why they had manipulated my father. I told them that I wouldn't be getting married just because they wanted to benefit from it. I put my foot down. "No!" I said. "I do not agree to this!"

We spent about two hours talking but I refused.

"My focus is on my education. That's all."

They now left it to Chris to persuade me. Chris used material possessions to try and convince me. "I'll buy you nice things if you come with me to Germany." But I resisted, saying that I could never pay him back anyway.

Later, I would discover that before Chris had visited the refugee camp, he had told most of his friends in Lusaka that he had gone to get a wife from Tanzania. So, everyone who saw me in Lusaka thought that I was dating Chris. That hurt a lot.

All I wanted now was to go back to school. After stopping school in the middle of the year because of the war in Burundi, Rwanda, and DR Congo, I had an aching hunger to continue my education.

Chris and Adam failed to entice me, so Chris decided to make another move. He asked Adam to pay him back the money he had used for my ticket from Tanzania. He also told him to move and rent somewhere else, and to pay back the money he had given Adam to start his small business.

Fighting for My Rights

Adam used the money from his grocery shop to repay Chris and paid two months of rent in advance for a new place. My sister and I left with Adam and his wife, and they became our host family as we moved from a middle-class area called Emmasdale to a poor area called Chaisa.

I remember our new landlord had a small TV and the day after we moved, we watched Princess Diana's funeral. I didn't really know who Princess Diana was, but I remember how I cried when I saw her beautiful face, her two young boys she had left behind, and when I heard how kind and generous she had been.

Life became tough for Adam. The shop looked empty because he had used the money to pay Chris back. I was blamed for everything. Adam started telling people, especially those from Rwanda and Burundi, that his shop had gone downhill because I had stolen and used his money. I didn't try to defend myself. I have always been a person who doesn't like to talk about my problems. I am someone who likes to fight to find solutions to my problems. It was at this point that I decided to fight for my rights too.

One day, I asked Adam when he thought my sister and I were going to be registered for school. Before he gave me an answer, he cleaned his throat. He was chewing some nuts. "Not until my shop gets back to where it was. It's empty because of you, so you have to stay in the shop selling groceries until things are better."

When I heard those words coming from a person I considered to be like a family member, it was like adding fuel to the fire of emotional abuse. I totally disagreed with him and told him that I was going to start going to an English school. I didn't care about what he was going to say behind my back, I wanted to find a school for me and my sister. All I could think about was my father in the refugee camp, hoping to receive a letter from us telling him that we had started going to school.

The next day, I asked my sister to sit with me and talk. She looked a bit scared and asked me what was wrong. I told her that I was going to school to learn English and that I had refused to stay in Adam's shop. I then told her my plan. "So, please, if you could stay in the shop all day, I will be going to learn English and when I come back from school I will join you in the shop and teach you what I have learned."

My sister agreed.

Adam knew none of this. He started flattering my sister, saying that she was a good girl with good manners, and that I was a bad girl with bad manners because I didn't submit to his wishes. I didn't care about what others were saying about me. I went to register for an English school at a place called Makeni.

I informed Adam that I was starting an advanced English course. Asking his permission was a waste of my time.

It was a 24 kilometre walk every day to and from school. When I got home, I would fetch my books and start teaching my sister about what I had learned. I wanted her to know some basic English words. She was only using the local language – Nyanja – which was more commonly used, especially if you spend all your time in a shop selling groceries.

The new academic year was going to start the following February (1998), so I wanted to do my best to ensure that I would be able to return to school. I took an intensive programme because I wanted to finish quickly and start looking for a place in a school for the next year.

In December 1997, a week before Christmas, I completed my English course. My Nyanja knowledge had also improved, and I was ready to fight for my rights and use both languages.

At home with Adam, I did everything that a girl must do. I cleaned the house, washed dishes, cooked, washed clothes, but still I was a bad girl in Adam's eyes. He kept trashing my reputation, claiming that I wasn't going to school, that I was going to see some boys, when I had not even kissed a boy. That really hurt me, but I stayed strong. I was only 17 years old.

We went to church most Sundays. The church was called Bread of Life. My sister and I enjoyed a good Christmas.

On New Year's Eve 1997, I heard fireworks for the first time. I will never forget how my sister and I ran and hid, thinking they were gunshots. I asked a lady if those were gunshots. She laughed before she answered me. I felt stupid. I didn't know why she thought it was so funny.

"No, those are fireworks," she said. "We do this every New Year's Eve. This is normal in Zambia. You must have lived in a country where there was a war."

"Yes," I said. "We were both traumatized by the sound of guns."

To this day, I still don't cope with fireworks.

God's Plan is Bigger!

In January 1998, I started looking for a school. My sister and I had already been given our refugee status which made the situation easier. I bought a green file in which to keep all the documents needed for us to be registered for school. I went every morning to the Ministry of Education to ask if there were any places. They took all of our details and they asked me to wait.

One day, I was walking back when I met a friend called Prime. He was also one of the Burundian refugee students in Lusaka. When he asked me where I'd been, I told him I had been trying to get a place somewhere in a boarding school. Boarding school was the best option. Living in Adam's place had become unbearable.

"You look tired," Prime said.

"I think it's because I am hungry," I said.

"I was going for my lunch. Do you want to come with me?" Prime asked.

"Sure."

We went downtown, found a restaurant, and ate meat pies.

"So, you said you want to go to a boarding school?" Prime said.

"Yeah, boarding school is better for us. We can practice our English with other students."

"Do you have sponsorship?"

"Not yet, but I was thinking of getting the application form."

"There is a priest called Father Aloyz," Prime said. "His office is at UNZA (the University of Zambia). If you tell him you are looking for a scholarship, maybe, if you are lucky, he will agree to sponsor you and your sister."

I asked him for the address and he wrote it down on a small piece of paper and told me how to get there and which bus to catch.

It was time for him to go back to his college but before he went, he gave me some money. "Buy some Fanta for your sister Annie," he said.

I said thank you.

Instead of continuing home, I went straight away to see Father Aloyz. I used the money Prime had given me, to buy Fanta to pay my bus ticket to UNZA. When I arrived, Father Aloyz was in his office. The door was open. I knocked on it.

"What can I do for you?" Father Aloyz asked.

"May I speak with you?"

He told me he was free and asked me to sit down.

"What's your problem?"

I sat on the chair and told him that I was looking for sponsorship for me and my sister, that I was still waiting for a response from the Ministry of Education about a place at a boarding school.

"Do you have parents?"

I replied that I was living with my host family and that my parents were not in Lusaka. He took all my details and my sister's and agreed to sponsor us if we managed to get places at a school.

I was overjoyed.

"Thank you so much!" I cried. "You have saved my life, and my sister's."

When I got home, I told my sister the good news and I asked her to keep it a secret, especially from Adam. A few days before, Adam had said that even if I could find a school place, I wouldn't find people to sponsor us because he had said bad things about me, giving me a bad name.

But God's plan was bigger than Adam's plan!

The Ministry of Education

At the end of January, I went back to the Ministry of Education to ask if there was any good news for me. They told me to return a week later. The schools were supposed to start in a week's time. I prayed that God would help, that there would be good news when I went back.

A week later, I returned.

"There's a place at a girl's secondary school at Chipembi in Kabwe Province," they said as I entered the office. The school's name is Chipembi Girls. It's two hours away from Lusaka."

They gave me the reference to take to the school and told me to talk with the headteacher there.

I went straight to Father Aloyz's office at UNZA and told him my sister and I had a place but that we didn't have a ticket to get us there. Father Aloyz gave me an envelope with money for the ticket and pocket money for my journey to Kabwe.

I went home and shared the good news with my sister. "Tomorrow I will be going to visit that school to get our acceptance letters."

I informed Adam that the next day that I was going to register for our new school in Kabwe. He looked at me and just shook his head. "And who do you think is going to agree to sponsor you?" he sniped.

"God," I answered.

I ran to see my sister in the grocery shop. I was so happy.

"You know what, sis?" I said. "We did not come to Lusaka to do business. We came here for a better education. I feel so bad that our father was deceived and manipulated, but I will fight until the end."

For a 17-year-old, I was now very responsible. My sister and I had been suffering an emotionally abusive life, but we hadn't given up. Members of the Burundi-Rwanda community in Zambia were bad-mouthing me. Most of them had a bad image of me because of what Adam had been saying. But I knew what I was up to and I didn't care at all. No one knew the story of Adam trying to force me to get married.

A Kind Headteacher

The next day, I took the bus and headed to Kabwe. I didn't realize that I had taken the wrong bus until I reached Kabwe city centre and asked the bus driver where Chipembi Girls School was. The school was in Kabwe Province but at a different location. No one had told me that there was a bus from Lusaka straight to my school.

"Oh my God!" I cried. "So, how can I get to Chipembi?"

The bus driver I was talking to was trying to finish his last cigarette.

"Well," he said, blowing the smoke from his cigarette, "you need to take another bus to a village where there are some trucks that pass near Chipembi Girls School. They can offer you a lift. That's the easiest way I know." Then he turned to another bus driver. "Hey man, are you full already?"

"We still have two places," the other driver replied.

I jumped on board. When we arrived, I went to speak to one of the women who sat in the shade of a tree selling tomatoes and onions.

"Do you know how I can get to Chipembi?

"Oh, my daughter! It's late now to get the truck passing Chipembi. The last one has just left."

I started to shake. "Oh, my God! What am I going to do?" I cried.

I was in an unfamiliar world in a village that looked very poor. I went to sit in the shade on the other side of the road. I looked desperate, like a chicken in the rain. I didn't know where I was. I had no phone to call for help, I really didn't know what to do.

An old man found me there and asked if I was okay.

"No, I'm not. I'm lost, and I need a place to sleep for the night."

"Wait here," the old man said. "I'll talk to someone and see if there is something they can do for you."

After few minutes, the old man came back with another guy.

"The only place is at a local primary school, in a security man's small room."

That scared me. What if someone tried to rape me? What will my sister think if I don't come back before nightfall? In the end, I felt I had no choice. They took me to the room, but I didn't close my eyes all night.

At 4 a.m., I heard the first sound of a chicken and an hour later birds chirping and singing. Slowly I began to feel my racing heart slowing down.

At about 6 a.m., the old man came to ask if I had a good night. I told him that it wasn't easy for me to sleep at a place I didn't know.

I had been so scared the night before I had lost my appetite. Now I was hungry, so I walked to the corner shop and bought some bread and juice for breakfast.

Around 10 a.m., the truck arrived, the one due to pass Chipembi Girls. The driver agreed to give me a lift and an hour later, we reached the school. The driver pointed to the entrance and I went straight to reception. A man who was standing outside directed me to the headteacher's office and there I was told to sit and wait.

Later, the door opened and the headteacher appeared.

It was the same man who had told me where the office was!

He invited me to come in. "So, my daughter. My name is Mr Dokowe. How can I help you?"

I introduced myself and told him that I really wanted a place for me and my sister at a boarding school. I explained the hard time I was having living at Adam's place and the whole story about him trying to force me to get married at such a young age.

The headteacher listened to me carefully, his glasses slipping down his nose. He fixed them back in place and sipped from the glass of water on his desk. It was very hot in January, and the ventilator wasn't blowing enough cool air into the office.

He was very shocked to hear my story. I cried several times and he tried to comfort me. Then he pulled out some forms from the drawers of his desk. He filled in the forms with my details and my sister's. Finally, he handed me two acceptance letters. My sister and I had been offered a place at his school! I cried tears of joy.

"It's okay," the headteacher said. "Go back to your sponsor and show him that you've got a place here, then come back next week to start school because others have already started few days ago."

I had said that I would never go down on my two knees to say thank you to someone, the way most Zambians did. But that day I went down on my two knees and thanked Mr Dokowe for saving our lives.

I walked out from the office to find that there was one bus outside which was going straight to Lusaka. That day, I knew that I had won the war. I had fought to get back to my education and I had conquered every obstacle.

I climbed on board the bus and headed back to Lusaka, looking at the two acceptance letters all the way back, checking to make sure our names where correctly written. As if a headteacher had written them wrongly!

Who's the Loser Now?

I arrived home in the middle of the afternoon around 3 p.m. My sister had not gone to the shop – she didn't feel well because she had not seen me returning home the previous night. When I entered the house, I said hello to everyone. Adam forced himself to answer me. My sister jumped up and gave me a big hug. She told me she had been so scared she couldn't sleep the night before.

I was still holding my green file with the two acceptance letters inside.

"So, what's the news?" my sister asked.

"I am sorry. I didn't find a place." I said, while Adam and his wife listened.

"I told you," Adam said, a fake smile on his face. "You won't find a school place until you give me my money back."

My sister looked disappointed and devastated but I didn't hint that I was hiding something. I just wanted to see Adam's reaction.

"I told you that I had a vision from God that you won't find a school, and even if you find one, you won't find sponsorship," said Adam, who always said he had visions from God when praying.

I looked at him and didn't say a word. What kind of a Christian was he, to treat someone the way he was treating us?

I didn't answer him. I just pulled the two acceptance letters from my green file. I showed them to my sister and told her that we were going to school just in a week time.

I will never forget my sister's reaction. I was her life-saver. I was rescuing her from being a shop assistant instead of being at school.

I told Adam that we had a sponsor already waiting to see our acceptance letter and that this meant we could get our school fees, pocket money and money to buy all we needed for school stuff.

Adam was in shock. He had nothing to say. He just walked into his bedroom. He had abused me verbally and emotionally. He had told my sister that I had gone to sleep with boys the night that I went to Chipembi Girls and my sister had started to believe him. He had now been found out. He was the loser.

Giving Myself a High-Five!

The next day, my sister and I went to see our sponsor Father Aloyz. I took our acceptance letters and I handed them to him. Father Aloyz made a copy of them and told us to wait. He went into the next room and brought two envelopes when he returned.

"Look," he said. "Your school fees. This is the money to buy all your school stuff and you should keep some for your school pocket money." The money was in Kwacha currency.

"You should learn how to save, because in the boarding school you will need some money to buy extra useful things, especially for you girls."

We gave Father Aloyz a big hug and thanked him. We cried tears of joy and when Father Aloyz had wiped our tears he said, "That's okay. From today you are my children. You will not miss out on anything. Just let me know whenever you need help."

More tears. When I looked behind where my sister was standing, I saw her wiping her face. She was crying too.

We left Father Aloyz's office, and as we walked through the corridor, I heard him calling us.

"Remember, you are now my children so do good at school, come back with good reports, otherwise I won't continue to sponsor you if you won't work hard."

We promised not to disappoint him.

We took the bus and went back home. Since I didn't know what was going to happen when we told Adam, I separated the money into two parts, putting the school fees and the pocket money together.

When we got home, we told Adam that we had come from meeting our sponsor.

"Where's the money?" he asked.

I lied to him. "We have only been given money to buy school stuff. The school fees and pocket money are being sent separately by Father Aloyz to the school."

"Give me the money," he said. I handed him the cash for the school items. But I had a plan in my head.

Late in the afternoon the next day, Adam told us to go downtown to do the school shopping.

"Do you have the money?" I asked him.

"Yeah, why?"

"Just asking," I said.

We arrived at the shopping centre and Adam entered a shop. I refused to follow him because I knew that they sold only cheap stuff and I also knew the amount of money in the envelope I had given him.

Adam kept asking me why I wasn't following him. I told him that I didn't want to buy our school materials there. "I think the other shop has more quality stuff," I said, pointing to another shop.

Adam had no idea about my plan.

I knew that he wanted to spend only half of the money so that he could pocket the rest. But I wasn't going to let him get away with that.

We went into another shop and Adam started pointing only to the cheap stuff. Then I started pointing to better items – a nice-looking suitcase, quality bedsheets, quality blankets, quality buckets, quality plates and spoons, quality notebooks – everything that had quality. I was calculating in my head. At the boarding school we had to provide most of what we needed to use there. In the dorms, all you had was a bed and mattress.

When we had finished ordering all the items, the shop assistant calculated the total and it was almost exactly the money that Adam had in his pocket. He had no choice but to pay the bill!

I had won again!

"How are we getting home with all this stuff?" Adam moaned.

"We will get a taxi," I said. "I think the remaining money can pay for that, right?"

It covered the fare exactly.

I had won again!

Even now, when I remember that day, I give myself a high-five!

This School is Your Home

That Sunday, we said goodbye to Adam and his wife. No one wished us good luck. No one escorted us to the bus station.

While seated on the bus, my sister beside me, I started thinking how wonderful it would be if our parents were there to accompany us so that they could see our new school. I was looking out the window, remembering all the ups-and-downs of fighting to get back into education. I closed my eyes and saw a very big door which was standing open. I immediately knew that we had started a new journey and that all the doors were open. I will always thank Father Aloyz for that and to this day I am still in touch with him. He is in Malawi and I always remember to say thank you. He had given us another chance in life. It was up to us to take it or waste it.

When we arrived, everything was new for my sister. We walked to the reception to report that we had arrived, but before we reached the receptionist, Mr Dokowe the headteacher recognized me.

"Oh, my daughters! Welcome! This is your school, but this is also your home."

He asked the secretary to register us and collect the school fees.

We gave our details and handed over the envelope with the school fees. My English wasn't fluent, but I could at least communicate. For my sister, it was harder.

We were then given a school tour and shown our dorms. The headteacher told us we would be see our classrooms the next day, on Monday.

I felt relieved. Other students were happy to meet us. We were a novelty because we came from a French educational system. They couldn't have been more welcoming or supportive.

The next day, it was our first school day in English. I was in Year 12 and my sister was in Year 9. It was a challenge, but we were ready to fight to overcome it. We wanted to make our father proud, even though at the time he didn't know we had managed to get a place there.

The first day was tough. I could hardly understand what the teacher was saying, but both students and teachers were helpful. I realized then that Zambian people are so lovely and good-hearted.

Students would come up and say, "I heard you are new and speak more French than English, right?" I would nod. "So where do you come from?"

"Um, from Burundi but I was born in Rwanda."

"Rwanda? How? And where is Burundi?"

"Burundi is in East Africa and Rwanda is the neighbouring country. My parents were refugees there when I was born."

"Good," they would say. "You will teach us French and we will teach you English."

There was one girl called Mathilda. She was one of my sister's friends and would translate books from Nyanja to English to help my sister understand the topic that they had learned that day.

You can only find a few people with a heart like that on this earth.

The Letter from my Father

I celebrated my eighteenth birthday at my new school during my first semester. I bought some drinks and scones for my classmates.

My sister and I were trying to work hard at school because we didn't want to disappoint Father Aloyz. I had not yet informed my parents that we had started school already nor had I explained how I had fought to get us there. Little did I know that they already had some fake news, until I saw a letter from my father.

Just a week before starting our two-week holiday, the receptionist told me that there was a letter for me. I thought it might be from Father Aloyz, asking me how it was going at school.

It was the week of our last exams before our first holidays.

After school time, I went to the reception to get my letter. I looked at the handwriting. "Oh my God! I exclaimed. "I recognize this handwriting. This is my father."

I was so excited. Then, before opening the envelope, I remembered that I hadn't told my father my school address, or even informed him that we were at school.

I had wanted to finish the first semester and see our school reports before writing to my parents.

Something felt wrong. I didn't want to open the letter alone. I wanted my sister beside me.

I went straight to my sister's dorm and showed her the envelope.

"Open! Open! Open!" my sister said, jumping with excitement.

The first thing I saw was a hand-drawn image of a tear. "Okay, let's read this," I said. We sat on my sister's bed and we started reading in silence.

It quickly became clear that it was Adam who had given him our school address. This meant he had sent a letter to my father telling him our news. The first line read, "I am so disappointed in you my children. You have broken my heart, especially Josée."

I still cry when I remember this.

The second line started with, "Adam told me."

There you go. What did he tell him? I wondered.

Adam had told my father that I had become a street girl and that I didn't do anything besides spending my time with boys.

I cried. I tried to hold it together and finish reading. In the end, I told my sister to keep the letter. I didn't want to take it to my dorm.

I went into my room, not wanting any of my roommates to see that I was hurt. I went straight to bed. It was time to go to the dining hall for our evening meal, but I didn't go. I wept under my bedsheets until I fell asleep. My sister came to check on me because she had not seen me in the dining hall, but she found me asleep.

In the middle of the night, I remembered the letter. I thought of the way my father had been deceived and

I could see how broken-hearted he was when writing that letter. I burst into tears again. I cried in silence, not wanting my roommates to hear.

The next day, I had my last English exam. I had not revised the night before, but I took a risk and sat for it. What surprised me was that I passed it with higher marks than my other exams.

Writing a Reply to my Father

Three days later, it was the end of the first semester and we went home for a two-week holiday. When we got there, we didn't find anyone at home. The house looked empty, as if the occupants had moved. As it turned out, Adam and the family had left. They just hadn't told us their new address.

There was one family friend of Adam also from Burundi and we went to ask them if they knew where Adam had gone. They pointed to a house around the corner. We were lucky we had only a small amount of stuff in our back bags. We had left our suitcases at school because it was just a short holiday.

We walked to the house and found Adam's wife sitting outside in the front yard. We greeted her. She looked happy to see us and I hoped Adam would have the same look on his face when he saw us. We asked her where her husband was so that we could say hi. She told us that he was inside.

We went in and greeted him politely. I acted as if we didn't know that he had contacted my parents.

We showed him our school results. He looked at them, but he didn't say a word.

The next day, the first thing we did was go and see Father Aloyz to show him our school report. We had really worked hard in a new English system and our results were amazing. After showing him, he gave us a big hug and congratulated us. Before we left, he gave us some money and asked us to return to get more pocket money three days before going back to school.

During that holiday with Adam, we went back to working in the shop. One day, when I was chatting with my sister there, I saw a familiar face. It was my father's friend, Bernardin. The last time I had seen him was in the refugee camp back in Tanzania. He had recently moved to Lusaka. He looked very happy to see us.

Bernardin said that he had a message from our dad. He told us that he was waiting for our holidays in Lusaka so that he could talk to me and my sister. Bernardin wanted to know how long we were staying in Lusaka before going back to school. He came every day to see us. He would find us at home, busy doing some housework, or he would come and find us at the shop. We had no idea that he was spying on us.

One day he asked my sister and I if we could go to visit him and his family. He had a wife and two young children. We said we would ask Adam for permission. Adam refused so we had to tell Bernardin that we were not allowed to go and visit him.

A few days later, we planned one afternoon to meet Bernardin and listen to what he wanted to tell us.

"You know, before moving to Lusaka from Tanzania, I went to say bye to your father and told him that I was coming to Lusaka. He told me about the letter he received from Adam with a lot of fake news about you girls. Your father has a broken heart because of the wrong information he has about you. Especially you Josée, your father is so disappointed in you. He said that he trusted you so much, but you disappointed him. But I have been observing you guys. Your father has totally wrong information about you. Please can you tell me what's going on so that I know what to tell your father."

At first, I asked myself if I should tell him the whole story. I asked my sister what she thought. In the end, because my father had told him how hurt and disappointed he was because of the fake news he had about me, I decided to tell him.

When I finished, he was shocked. "You should immediately send a letter to your father and explain everything," Bernardin said.

"I was actually preparing to do it before we returned to school," I said.

That night, I waited until Adam and his wife went to bed. I sat down in the living room and I wrote until my fingers started hurting. The more I wrote, the more I cried. The letter ran to eight A4 pages. I shared everything.

The Three Girls from East Africa

Three days before going back to school for our second semester, we went to get our school pocket money. When we got to Father Aloyz's office, we found a young lady my sister's age waiting to talk to him. She was also looking for sponsorship. She said her name was Marie Louise, but we could call her Louise.

"Are you looking for sponsorship?" Louise asked us.

"No, we are already sponsored by Father Aloyz," I replied. "How about you?" I asked.

"Well, not yet. He promised to sponsor me, but I want to go to boarding school."

"Why can't you come to our school in Kabwe?" My sister asked.

She was impressed with the idea and I told her how I got the place and who she should ask to help her at the Ministry of Education. She said that she was going to try to go there the next day.

We wished her good luck in her school hunting and we told her that we hoped she would come to Chipembi Girls.

That day, Father Aloyz, gave us our pocket money. It was more than enough. I don't know how I got the idea of saving money, but I started putting money aside even though I didn't have any plan for it.

Three weeks later, after we had returned to school, we saw Louise at reception holding a big suitcase. I called my sister and pointed to Louise. We rushed and gave her a hug. She was joining Chipembi Girls, so there were now three girls from East Africa, because Louise also came from Rwanda.

From that day, we told other students we were related and that she was our cousin. We started as best friends and we ended up being sisters. We had a powerful connection between us. We did everything together, plus we had the same sponsor. To this day she is still our sister and we can't spend a week without talking to her. Louise is still in Zambia.

My Father's Apology

We enjoyed being at Chipembi Girls. Our English was improving. I had joined the school club activities and I played volleyball. My sister joined the athletics team.

One day, in the middle of our exams, I passed reception to see if there were any letters for me. There were two. I could see from the handwriting that one was from my father; the other said on the back of the envelope that the sender was Adam.

I wanted to open my father's letter first, so once again I went to see my sister in her dorm so that we could read it together. This time I didn't cry because I was hurt. I cried because I was overjoyed.

My father apologized for the letter he had sent to me before, saying he was so sorry that he made me cry, that it was because he cared, but that he was disappointed to read what Adam had said. The thing that touched me most was this: "I just want you to act as diplomatic people. Even if Adam says untruths about you, just accept that you did it so that you can find a place to stay. Remember, I told you home is always home and you are not at home. Firstly, you are in a foreign country. Secondly, you are at people's place. Accept even if you didn't do it, to avoid being homeless." This message was very challenging to me – very, very, very challenging. But I had no choice but to follow my father's advice.

Then I opened the second letter and read it with my sister. In it, Adam said: "Hope you guys are doing great at school. Us we are all okay. I just wanted to let you know that I don't want to see you back at my house when you come for the next holiday. Just find another place where you can go."

How was I to react to these two different letters? As for me, I became as strong as a rock. I was doing my exams and there were two weeks left before finishing them.

My sister, on the other hand, panicked. She was terrified and kept asking me where we were going to live.

"You know what, sis?" I said. "Let's concentrate on our exams and make sure we pass them."

Thereafter, if I met my sister at the dining hall, she would ask me, "Jo where are we going to live?"

"With Adam," I would answer.

If she came to my dorm, she would ask me the same question and I would give her the same answer.

After a while, I started avoiding her. We didn't tell Louise our problem even though she was our friend. She was new at school and we were still getting to know each other, so my sister and I kept it to ourselves.

We finished our exams and passed all of them. The second semester was now over. Two days before we left on our next two-week holiday, I was sitting with my sister telling her that we had no other choice but to go to Adam's place, and that I didn't want to stress myself by thinking about it again.

The day came to leave school. There were so many buses taking students to Lusaka. Everyone was asking why we were not boarding the bus to go home. We answered that we had not yet received our ticket from our sponsor. Louise had her ticket and I lied to her that we had used the money for our ticket to buy some school stuff. I also told her that I had asked my English teacher if I could borrow some money and I was waiting for her to give it to me. Louise was so worried about us, but I assured her that we were going to be fine. She took the bus and went home, but she looked unhappy that she had left us behind.

We stayed there staring at other students who were excited about going back home on their holidays.

My sister and I wished our parents were living in Zambia at that moment. We didn't know what to do.

We took the very last bus and reached Lusaka around 6 p.m., when it had started getting dark. We had to connect to another bus to take us to Chaisa where Adam lived, but my sister and I were hesitating. The only option was to take a risk and see if Adam was going to chase us away.

When we got to Adam's place, my sister said, "You knock first. You are the oldest."

I knocked.

I saw Adam looking through the window.

He opened the door and stared at us.

"How are you? What do you want?" Adam asked.

"Fine thanks. And you?" I asked.

He just shook his head. "Did you receive my letter?"

"Yes."

I wanted to say 'no' but decided to tell the truth.

"So, what are you doing here?" he asked.

"We had nowhere else to go." I was doing all the talking. My sister was hiding behind me.

"I told you that no one around here will ever take you in," Adam said.

I was stuck. There was nowhere else to turn.

"Do you accept all the mistakes you've made?" Adam asked. Before I answered, I remembered the last letter my father had sent, where he said that I should accept Adam's criticisms even if they weren't true.

So, I nodded. Adam then gave us conditions and rules to follow before he would accept us inside his house. First, I had to wake up 5 a.m. in the morning and go to the bread wholesale. Second, we had to stop going to our normal church and go to his. Third, we had to wear long clothes – no short skirts, no clothes with short sleeves, no trousers, no shorts. Fourth, my sister and I had to spend all day selling bread at the roadside. Fifth, there was to be no asking permission to visit someone.

The next day he brought us new clothes that we had to wear. I woke up 5 a.m. in the morning every day and went to buy bread and spent all day sitting at the roadside selling it with my sister. We only ate once a day, but we could use the little money that I was saving to buy something to eat. We felt like prisoners.

At last, the 'holiday' finished and we went back to school for our final semester. My sister and I passed our end of the year exams and we had good results, so we were able to move up to the next school year.

We went home for our long, two-month summer holiday during Christmas 1998 and New Year 1999. During our holiday, we continued following Adam's rules and conditions. Just before Christmas, we told Adam that we were going to see Father Aloyz and take a Christmas card for him. Going to see Father Aloyz was breaking one of the conditions that he had given us.

"I told you, no asking permission for going somewhere," Adam said.

Ignoring Adam, we went that day, but Father Aloyz wasn't in his office. We went back home and decided to return another day. My sister and I didn't know that we were going to be homeless the next day.

Out on the Streets

Late in the evening, before we went to bed, Adam called us and said that he wanted to talk to us. We went and stood in their bedroom. "I need your things out of my house by tomorrow around 12 p.m.," he said.

I didn't look surprised or unhappy. I couldn't quite take it in, so I asked if he meant our things or us. He looked as if he was going to shoot me.

"I need things and people out of my house by tomorrow at 12 p.m."

My sister and I didn't cry. We just went outside and laughed. Everything was beyond our comprehension so all we could do was laugh.

The next day, by 12 p.m., we had packed our things and left Adam's house. There were no homes or shelters for the homeless. We approached a man who had a grocery shop and asked him if he could keep our suitcases for us. We told him that we were coming to retrieve them later in the evening.

We had no idea what to do. Most of the Burundian and Rwandan community had a bad picture of me because of Adam's slander. We didn't know where Bernardin lived. My sister and I were homeless.

We spent all day in the town centre, window shopping, going here-and-there. It was 24 December and we were waiting for nightfall so that we could spend our Christmas Eve in church. There was a church service until three in the morning.

That evening, we sang Christmas songs, watched Christmas movies and, at around three in the morning, the service ended, and everyone left. My sister and I looked at each other wondering where to go now.

"Wait," I said. "Let me show you what to do."

I remembered the time I went to Kabwe and spent the night in the security man's house, and so I talked to the security guard. I told him what happened to us. He was happy to give us a place to sleep until 7 a.m.

The next morning, we didn't even attend the Christmas Day service. We just went downtown and walked around the area called Kanyama where Bernardin had told us he lived. Luckily, I saw a guy from Burundi and he directed us to Bernardin's place.

Bernardin and his family were living a tough life; they had moved into a big city from the refugee camp in Tanzania, so it was hard for them. We told them that we were homeless, and they agreed to give us a place to stay. We had one month before going back to school. That was our worse Christmas ever.

The next day was my sister's seventeenth birthday and it passed in silence. We lived simply, like other normal days. We were heartbroken and had no idea what the future held.

Then, later that month and in the middle of the night, I was lying awake. I had failed to get to sleep and had started thinking. I was staring at the ceiling and images were passing through my head. I was trying to figure out our next step.

Suddenly, I had an idea. I had become very responsible at a young age and that, like my father, I was capable of quick and decisive action. Anyway, my idea was to go straight to college instead of looking for a job. I would have my own room at college and could stay there all the time, even during holidays. I wanted to be independent and yet also be responsible for my younger sister. That's what my father had asked me to do, to take care of her.

At the beginning of 1999, I went to the Ministry of Education and I talked to someone in charge of the admission cases for college. I talked to him and explained my situation. I told him that I wanted to do journalism at Evelyn Hone College. He looked for me but said there were no places for journalism. It had been always my dream since I was a young girl to become a journalist.

I asked if there was any other course. He showed me the courses available at another college called Lusaka Trade. I picked administration.

I went to see Father Aloyz and told him my plan. I shared what had happened to us and he said that it was okay, that he was going to continue sponsoring me. He had no place to put us because he was living in a community residence with other priests.

I was still waiting for my school exam results. When they came, I had passed them all. I jumped to my feet and thanked God. I then told Bernardin that I was going to college and I would be staying there during holidays so that my sister could have a place during her holidays too.

Free at Last from Adam's Abuse

The day the college opened, I went to talk to the headteacher and explained about being homeless. I told him I wanted to stay on campus so that when my sister was on her holidays she could be with me at the college. I didn't want to tell my parents that we were homeless, that Adam had chased us from his place, but when I got a place at college I immediately sent a letter to my parents to let them know that we were no longer living at Adam's house.

My sister went back to Chipembi Girls and I went to college. I knew that my sister had Louise, that she wouldn't feel lonely, and I would visit them often.

I had never felt free in my life like the way I did in February 1999. I was no longer suffering Adam's emotional abuse. The smile had returned to my face.

One day, I was walking downtown trying to do buy some things for my kitchen. I didn't like the food they cooked at college and I wanted to cook for myself. Father Aloyz had given me enough money to buy everything I needed for college.

When I came out from one shop, I bumped into an old childhood friend called Fanny. We almost fell over hugging. I asked her where she lived, and she told me she was a student at the college where I wanted to do journalism – Evelyn Hone College – and she was also staying at the school campus. We promised to visit each other and from that time we became inseparable. She was my best friend and she visited me at college. I visited her at her college and most of the time we went together to her church where we could have lunch together after the service with her family. Her parents and her brothers were also living in Lusaka. She was the only girl out of six boys! I was like her younger sister.

We went clubbing and shopping, we went to parties and did all kinds of stuff together. I had learned how to save money from my sponsorship, so we could use some of my money to enjoy life.

We had another friend called Patty and she joined in with most of the things we did. During holidays, my sister would come and spend her holiday with me in my room at college. Even though we had no proper home we didn't have to worry about Adam anymore.

My First Boyfriend

My sister and I started gaining a bit of weight and we looked healthy and stress-free. My nineteenth birthday I celebrated at the college with my roommate Brenda.

I really had a nice time at college. I couldn't remember the last time I had felt the way I did then. Myself, Fanny, Patty, my sister, and Louise would go clubbing most of the weekends during holidays.

Later, I started dating Frankie, one of Fanny's brothers. He was my first boyfriend and it was a new experience for me. I had been always careful and scared to date someone. I had obeyed my father's advice about being careful with boys. I thought, maybe this time, I would give it a try. We were young and in love. I was 19 and he was four years older than me. It didn't last though. He was more like a brother to me. I was still young but because of what I had gone through, I had become an adult by force. I knew he was still playing around with other girls, so I decided to end it before my heart was broken. Sometimes I would hear knocking on my door at the college and it was Frankie. Of course, I would let him come in, but we always found ourselves kissing again. It was crazy.

I decided to end it completely and started avoiding him, which was hard because I visited their house so often. I would go with Fanny for sleepovers and spend weekends at her parents. But at last I managed to put it aside and move on.

How about South Africa?

In the middle of June, I received a letter from my father. He was encouraging us to be strong and keep our faith in God. He was so sad to hear what had happened to us, the way we had become homeless. He felt like he had abandoned us.

Before my sister and I had gone to Lusaka, my father had suggested that they might also move to Lusaka, but in the letter, he told me that it wasn't possible for them to move, because he was involved in the Burundi Peace and Reconciliation hosted by President Nelson Mandela in Arusha, Tanzania. I knew that he always believed in negotiating for peace in Burundi, so it was a big opportunity for him to represent people who were in exile during the Burundi Peace Negotiation.

In July, during the holidays, my sister was with me and most of the students had gone home. Only a few of us had remained at college. Something strange happened. In the middle of the night, I heard people knocking hard on our door.

"Open up or we will get in by force," two guys were shouting.

"Oh, my God," I thought.

They were about to break open the door when help arrived, and the police arrested them. The security men outside had warned them. We opened the door, which was damaged, and the police asked us to leave.

"Don't you have relatives here?" the policeman asked.

"No, we are refugees in Zambia and we don't have anywhere to live during our holidays." I was crying as I spoke.

From that day, the security service was improved, but my heart was no longer at peace. I was sure those guys wanted to rape us. We were in danger.

The following day, we went to see Father Aloyz and told him about the incident. He also looked worried but didn't know what he could do. He gave us our pocket money and we went back to the college praying that nothing bad would happen again. At that time, Louise was also having some misunderstandings with her family and she came to stay with us. Our nights became sleepless and, as usual, I started planning what to do for us to stay safe, but I really had no ideas this time.

Several weeks later, I received a letter from my uncle (my mother's brother) who was living in South Africa. This uncle had never met me. I grew up in Rwanda and he grew up in Burundi. I only knew him from pictures and letters. When I had gone to Burundi to meet my family, the war started two days before he had promised to come and see me at school. In his letter he sent me his phone number and asked me to call him.

Some Somalians had an international calling shop, so I went to phone my uncle. We talked for about twenty minutes. I briefly tried to explain about our life situation in Lusaka, and he was so sad to hear that we were homeless.

"Why can't you guys come down to South Africa?" he asked.

"How can we? We have no travel documents. I hear it's hard to get there, but I will think about it," I said.

Later, my mind returned to this conversation. I didn't say a word to my sister, or to Louise, but I kept planning. I decided that we should try to move to South Africa, but first I had another idea.

I thought about the refugee camp where my parents and my brothers were living, and I didn't see any future for my two brothers. I knew that there was no chance for my parents to move to Lusaka, since my father had started a new commitment to fight for peace. I would first go back to Tanzania and bring my brothers over to Zambia and then move to South Africa. I knew that would be an adventure, so I started planning for the journey. It wasn't going to be easy. I still had to know how I would travel, how I would cross the border, and how I would find travel documents.

One day, I met my friend Jocelyne and told her about my plan. She gave me some information about how I could get a Zambian travel document to use to get to Tanzania. She also told me how I could pass through Mozambique if I wanted to go to South Africa. She had all the information and connections. I asked her to give me the connection for gaining a Zambian travel document and she wrote everything down for me. I had money and I could get one easily.

Two days later, I went to meet a guy downtown who was going to help me find a Zambian travel document. We sat in a restaurant, ordered some food and talked. This time, corruption was going to play a big part in getting a Zambian travel document.

"Give me $100 and I'll get you a travel document."

I gave him half and told him that I would give him the rest after he had brought me the papers.

Two weeks later, he called me and asked if we could meet at the same place. I went downtown and we met in the same restaurant. He showed me that it was a genuine document and I gave him the remaining $50.

My name on that document was shown as Sharon Banda. Banda is one of the common names in Zambia, especially for those from Chipata who speak proper Nyanja. I could speak it fluently.

I planned to make my journey in September 1999.

It was time to take risks.

Me in Cairo – Egypt. I was living a dream. (July 2009)

Me, my brother Lambert and my sister Annie in
Brussels – Belgium. (November 2013)

Chapter 10
HERE COMES THE FLOOD

I headed to Mpulungu and waited for the boat to Kigoma, spending the night in one of the bed and breakfast places there. I spoke only in English and Nyanja because I had a Zambian travel document.

The next day, I went to the immigration office. The official studied me carefully. He looked at my picture, then spoke to me in Nyanja. I answered in the same language. Then he spoke to me in English and once again I answered him, this time in English. He stamped my document. "Safe journey," he said. My first step was complete.

I went outside and walked towards the boat, thanking God under my breath. I had made it through Zambian immigration. When I boarded the boat, I saw that I had boarded the boat I boarded two years ago when coming to Zambia.

I met two guys from Burundi on the boat who were also travelling to Tanzania. I wasn't supposed to talk in my own language while I was in possession of a Zambian document. One of them came and spoke to me in Kirundi but I reacted as if I didn't understand. Then he changed to French. Again, I acted dumb.

One of them said, "This lady looks East African – from Burundi or Rwanda."

Oh my God, I cried silently. I didn't say a word, and I didn't act as if I was listening to their words. I was praying for God to help me and to remove these guys. I didn't want to be the first to walk away; they might have thought I was trying to avoid them. Neither of them was speaking Nyanja or English, just French or Kirundi. I heard everything they said but I didn't want to show that I understood.

After three days on the boat, we finally reached Kigoma. I managed to pass through immigration and entered Tanzanian territory without any problem. I took a deep breath. I had made it! My second step was complete.

A Responsible Young Lady

I knew that my father was in a meeting in Arusha, so I went downtown and sent a fax to him, saying that I was on my way to the camp and I was going to stay for only ten days because I had to go back to college. I asked him when the meeting was going to finish. I wanted to know if I could see him before going back to Zambia.

A few hours later, I took the bus to the refugee camp. When I arrived, no one knew I was coming. I went straight to where my mother was teaching. She almost fainted when she saw me. I went to see my young brother Deo in his class and he couldn't believe I was there; he thought he was dreaming. If he had known that I was going to get him out of that forest, he would have jumped so high he would have touched the sky.

Luckily enough, my father was already done with the meeting and now had to return to the camp. When he saw my fax message, he flew immediately to Mwanza and then went by road to the camp.

I had already spent two days there and in the afternoon, I was sitting outside reading my book. It was then that I saw my father coming home. I ran to hug him. It had been two years since I had seen him.

"A long time ago," my father said, "I told you that you were a girl of adventure." He looked so delighted and happy to see me.

"If you knew how I got here," I said, "you would definitely say I am a girl of adventure."

I told him that I had used a Zambian document. I showed it to him. He started using the name on my papers and calling me Sharon! I had really missed him.

The next day I got straight to the point and told my parents I wanted to take my brothers Lambert and Deo with me back to Zambia. I shared with them my plan to go to South Africa. My father was very impressed, he couldn't believe how his little girl had grown into a responsible young lady. They said they would think about it and give me an answer. I was only going to be there another four days, so I needed to know their decision.

The next day, my father and I took a walk and he told me that they had decided to let my brother Lambert go with me back to Zambia. He said that they didn't want to remain alone without a child, so Deo would stay with them. I was okay with that; they had at least agreed to let one of my brothers go with me.

The same night, my dad sat with my brother and informed him that in three days' time he was going to leave the camp and go with me to Zambia. I will never forget what my father said to me.

"You have now got a very big responsibility. You need to take care of your sister and your brother. These are your children now. You are the father and the mother of your siblings, even if you still need someone also to take care of you. But I trust you and that's why I am giving you this responsibility. Try everything you can to reach South Africa or Europe for a better education, and don't leave your brother and sister behind."

I was speechless. I had no idea that my father trusted me enough to act in their place as parents. I was only 19 years old. Both my parents blessed us and prayed for us to have a safe trip.

A Generous Priest

Two days later, I cried like a baby when I said goodbye to my parents and Deo. I didn't know if I would ever see them again.

My brother Lambert and I headed to Kigoma where I arranged for a Tanzanian travel document to be issued to him. This time we took a different boat to the one I had boarded on my way to Tanzania.

Three days later we reached Mpulungu. I had a Zambian document, my brother a Tanzanian document. There was a guy from Tanzania and we had spent several days chatting with him on the boat. I asked him if he could walk into the immigration office with Lambert and say that he was his brother. I told him I would give him some money if he did. At first, he hesitated, but when he heard about the money, he quickly accepted. In the end, I had been scared for no reason. The immigration officers didn't ask my brother a single question! However, I kept my promise and gave the guy $15.

We took a bus and headed to Lusaka. I had arranged a place for my brother to stay with some students from Burundi. I took him there, then went back to college.

The next day, I went to see Father Aloyz with my brother.

"What can I do to help?" Father Aloyz said.

"I need to do some clothes shopping for my brother here," I replied.

Father Aloyz gave me some money, and as we went back home, we passed some time buying new clothes for Lambert. He had come from the refugee camp, and all his clothes looked very old.

We always received money from Father Aloyz because he was our sponsor. I wasn't working; I was still a student, so the only income I had was from him, and it helped us a lot. Most of the time, girls (especially in Africa or other less fortunate countries) go into prostitution because they don't have money to take care of themselves. Some of them even get pregnant and end up being miserable when they have been abandoned by their families or by those who made them pregnant.

We were so blessed to have Father Aloyz. He provided everything we needed.

Classy, Clean and Intellectual!

"Guys, what do you think about another adventure – the three of us moving to South Africa?" I asked my siblings. At first, they looked at me as if I was crazy. I had not told them that the next plan was to move to another country.

"How are we going to get there?" my sister asked.

"Just tell me if you are all cool with that and I will tell you."

"I am cool with that," my brother said.

"Me too, if you are sure about that," my sister added.

I had no time to waste so I started planning. My friend Jocelyne had told me about some trucks which transported copper to Mozambique. They offered lifts to people who wanted to cross the border. Passing through Mozambique was the easiest and safest way to get to South Africa.

Jocelyne showed me the offices where I could talk to one of the managers in charge of the trucks that went to a place called Beira in Mozambique. When I arrived, there were a lot of people, mostly women, sitting at the front of the big gate waiting to talk to the truck drivers to get a lift to Chipata, a place that the trucks passed before crossing the border to Mozambique. When I looked at the crowd, I realized that it wasn't going to be easy to talk to the manager. I didn't want to talk to the drivers like the people sitting outside. I wanted to go straight to the manager. He could connect me with someone he trusted.

To reach the manager's offices, you had to pass through a big gate guarded by security. You had to be working there to be allowed access. How was I going to do that? Then I had an idea.

I went back to college, took some money and went downtown to the shopping centre. I bought an office outfit for myself – a nice blazer, smart skirt, high heel shoes – and returned to college.

The next day, I put on the outfit, picked up an office briefcase, and made my way to the gate and to the manager's offices. I had already watched how other employees were entering the gate the day before. When I got there, I passed through that gate as if I was one of the employees. The security man didn't realize that I wasn't working there. I looked classy, clean, and intellectual!

When I got to reception, I asked if I could speak to one of the managers. The receptionist offered me a place to sit and, a few minutes later, one of the managers came and asked me to follow him into his office.

I explained the story of my life in Zambia. I didn't tell him that I was moving to South Africa. I told him that we wanted to go to Mozambique to visit a family member we had not seen for a long time. He felt sorry that we were homeless, that I had to stay at college because we didn't have a place called home. "Let me find you a driver who I trust," he said.

He called one of the truck drivers and told him that he needed to take care of us until we reached Mozambique. The agreement was that we would each pay $50 to the driver when we got there. He also asked me to bring him some photo ID of myself, my brother and my sister. I had these with me in my purse so I handed them to him.

$50 was okay because I had planned for at least $100 each. We agreed the price and fixed the date to leave. He told me that the trucks always left Lusaka around 1 p.m.

A Friend's Wedding

That same evening, I went to see Father Aloyz. "We have decided to leave Zambia," I told him. "It's becoming dangerous for us and we are living a hard life at our young age. I have arranged for the transport and we are leaving in a month."

It was very hard for him to understand, but he had no place for us; he was living with other priests at their residence, so his only option was to help us. I had already planned everything. My uncle had agreed to rent a big house in South Africa where we would stay with him. He was single and he wanted to get to know us better.

"Stay in touch," Father Aloyz said. "I will connect you with other Jesuit priests when you arrive. Just let me know your address."

He then gave me some money for our journey.

We told very few people we were leaving. Louise knew about it. She was devastated to hear that we were leaving her, but at least she had her big sister in Lusaka. The only other person I wanted to tell was Fanny. I also told my other friend Jocelyne, the one who had given me all the information about how I could get the transport for our journey.

When, I went to see Fanny at her room at college, she was also planning to come and see me. She said that she had something she wanted to tell me. "I'm getting married soon and I want you to come to my wedding."

"Oh my God!" I said. "I have to leave Lusaka. I don't think I can make it."

"No way! You have to serve me at my table because I don't trust those other girls. They might put something in my drink or food."

I would now have to wait. Fanny was more than a sister to me.

The day after her wedding, my sister and I went to stay for a week at Fanny's new house. We helped unpack her wedding gifts and redecorate her house.

Broken Down

On 11 December, my sister Annie, my brother Lambert and I left Lusaka. We had been at the place to meet our driver by 12:30 p.m. I didn't know how we were going to cross the border, but I did know that the driver was going to arrange everything. We had only one suitcase and the briefcase that my father had bought in Switzerland. I had told my siblings that we didn't have to take a lot of stuff.

After we had spent eight hours in the truck, we finally reached Chipata, not far from where we had to cross the border into Mozambique territory. The truck stopped and we all got out.

"What's going on?" I asked the driver.

"I think the truck has broken down. We are going to have to spend a night in Chipata," he replied.

A night in Chipata? I thought.

"Don't worry," he said. "I will arrange a safe place for you guys to sleep. You are now my responsibility. I have to take care of you guys."

One night became three weeks. We stayed with a lovely Zambian family related to our truck driver. We even spent Christmas and New Year with them. It was the first time we had met, but it felt like we had known them for ages.

There was one boy aged about 15 in Chipata. He wore the same outfit every day. It had holes in it and he had no other clothes. My brother took a few of his clothes and gave them to him. What touched me was how that boy went down on his knees and thanked my brother, who quickly pulled him back up to his feet. It was normal for the boy to do this within his culture, but it wasn't necessary.

New Year's Eve 1999, everyone was panicking, saying that the year 2000 would be the end of the world. But we finished 1999 and entered 2000 without any crisis. The world was the same as it had been before.

The week after New Year's Day, we were informed that our truck was fixed. We were now ready to continue to Mozambique. We thanked the family that had looked after us for almost a month and we climbed on board.

When we got to the border, the driver said, "Look guys. These are your travel documents. I will take them to get stamped. You stay inside the truck. Don't go outside. Let me take care of everything." I knew that he had everything under control, so I didn't ask him any more questions.

Our driver entered the Zambian immigration to get an exit visa and came back holding our documents in his hands. I don't know how we got those documents; I had given our photo passports to the manager and he had arranged everything. We had got through the Zambian border control okay. Now I started to believe we could get through the Mozambique one and begiven our entry visas. But I was wrong.

It was now around 8 p.m. and the driver told us that he was taking us to a place where we would sleep until 3 a.m. At One o'clock, I awoke in the dark in a strange room and we were brought to a place like a pub, with adjoining rooms. We were given one room to sleep in and the co-driver said he would wake us up later.

These truck drivers were used to that area and always took people who didn't have travel documents, especially refugees. Later, I came to learn that those documents the driver had for us were only to cross the Zambian border, not to enter Mozambique.

A Real Adventure

At around 2:45 a.m., we were awakened from a deep sleep. We went outside in the dark and followed the co-driver. He asked us not to talk and to remove our shoes. We could hear the immigration officers and security guards chatting a few metres away. The co-driver showed us a big wooden barrier separating the Zambian and Mozambique borders. "Pass under it," he whispered. There were no street lights in that village.

During the day, there were always people to open the barrier so that the cars could pass. At night there would be security guards to watch out for refugees crossing the border. For some reason there was no security and we passed easily through the border.

We were now on Mozambique territory and we walked about 3 kilometres to a place where the co-driver asked us to wait until 6 a.m. I was on a great adventure again, but this time I had my brother and sister with me.

We went into a small house full of tyres and petrol containers. The co-driver told us that it was where they kept extra supplies for the truck, not far from the border. He showed us a place to sleep and gave us two blankets – one to sleep on and the other one to cover ourselves.

"Oh God!" I said to my siblings. "This is a real adventure, I swear to God."

"Hey guys," the co-driver said. "Don't talk. The house next door is occupied by immigration officers. If they find you here, they will ask for your travel documents and we will all be in trouble."

We quietened down and lay on our blankets, but when we tried to sleep, we heard something moving.

"Did you hear that?" I whispered.

"Yeah," both my sister and brother said at the same time.

"What is it?" my brother asked.

It was then that we saw them – mice running all over the place. We were all scared, but none of us could scream. We stayed up, our eyes wide open.

A few hours later, it started getting lighter outside. We looked through a window with a curtain and saw where our truck was parking. At 6:10 a.m., it started moving in our direction.

"What if they just leave us here and go?" I asked.

They both looked at me as if I was being crazy.

A few minutes later, the truck parked outside. The driver and co-driver changed the oil, put air in the tyres, and then asked us to get back on board. From there, we headed without incident to a place called Tete. We arrived at 6 p.m., ten hours later. We had a lot of stops on our way, sometimes for refuelling, sometimes for eating. We stopped once when the truck broke down, at other times simply to get a rest.

On the journey we listened to tapes of Michael Jackson's songs and Congolese music that I had received from my father when I left Tanzania. We gave them to the driver to play while we took a rest or when we stopped to eat. When the truck broke down, the music provided light relief and we sometimes even danced to make it more fun.

We often stopped at places where truck drivers cooked food for themselves instead of buying from the restaurants. My sister and I usually cooked the food and we would all sit under the shade of a tree and have our meal – the driver, co-driver, myself, my brother and my sister. It was a great adventure.

One Good Deed

In this new world, apart from the driver and the co-driver who spoke in English, everyone else spoke in Portuguese. I wasn't that bothered because the plan was to get to Maputo, the capital city of Mozambique, and then continue to South Africa where I could communicate easily in English.

We spent two nights in Tete because it had been raining heavily for two days. When the rain had calmed down, we left Tete and headed to Beira, where we had to connect with our transport to take us to Maputo. While we approached Beira, we noticed buildings that had been destroyed during the war in Mozambique. There were bullets on the ground, weapon pieces too, and old, huge military trucks that had been used during the war.

Around 1 p.m., we reached Beira Port, the destination for all the trucks with copper from Zambia. By now we had spent almost two months with the driver. It was 25 January when we finally reached Beira.

I paid the driver for the journey and thanked him for taking care of us. When I handed the $150 to him, he refused to take it. At first, I was scared that maybe he was going to charge us more but instead he told me that they wouldn't have been able to endure the long journey from Lusaka to Beira if it wasn't for all our entertainment!

"You guys are so amazing," he said. "I have never driven people like you since I started doing this job. I have always had bad experiences with rude people, but you guys have been a blessing to me. I wish you all the best and please, when you come back, just let me know so that I can take you back to Lusaka."

I was so touched. Before we had left Lusaka, I had told his manager that we were going to Mozambique to visit our family. I didn't tell them that we were moving to South Africa. I wanted to protect ourselves as young refugees. In Beira, I tried to call my uncle in South Africa, using a public phone around the corner from where the truck was parked, but he wasn't picking up. I called his friend in Maputo who was supposed to pick us up. He didn't pick up either. I called each of them more than ten times. Finally, I gave up.

There was one bus due to leave Beira for Maputo, and it was going to leave at 3 p.m. The truck driver helped us to buy the tickets because he spoke Portuguese. While we waited for the bus, we saw a young man who was crying like a baby. My siblings and I decided to approach him and asked him what was wrong. He told us that he had come from Malawi, just like we had from Zambia, but he was having a problem paying the driver who had helped him to cross the border.

"How much do you have to pay?" I asked.

"$100, but I only have $50. I had money when I left Malawi, but I used it because we spent more days there than I expected." He was struggling to speak English, so we asked him which language he could speak better. I knew that he was going to say French because he spoke English with a French accent.

"Where do you come from?" my sister asked.

"My name is Jimmy and I am from Congo DRC."

Jimmy was also travelling to Maputo on his way to South Africa.

"Wait a second Jimmy," I said. "Let me talk to my siblings and see what we can do for you."

We chatted for a moment and agreed to help him with the $50. We had not paid the $150 we were supposed to pay our driver, so we gave some of it to someone who really needed a helping hand.

We went back to Jimmy who was sitting on the ground looking hopeless. We gave him the $50 and we bought his coach ticket to Maputo.

Around 3 p.m., we boarded the same bus for the 1,200-kilometre journey from Beira to Maputo and arrived there the next morning around 10 a.m. We said goodbye to Jimmy and said that we hoped to meet him one day in South Africa.

Back to Camp

Everyone in Maputo spoke Portuguese. My siblings and I stood at one corner watching everyone minding their own business in the city. No one realized that we were strangers there because Maputo had different nationalities. It was confusing!

We started laughing, not because we had gone crazy, but because we didn't know what to do next. We didn't know where to start or which language to use. You could say, "Excuse me," but no one reacted!

I had promised my uncle in South Africa that I was going to call him once we reached Maputo, so he would know we had arrived safely. I also had to call his friend who was supposed to come and pick us up. But what language was I going to use when asking someone if there wasn't a public phone nearby? I even considered using sign language.

As I was still figuring out what to do next, I heard a man ending a conversation on the phone and he was saying goodbye in English.

"Wait a second!" I said to my siblings. "I just heard someone speaking English!"

I rushed to where the man was standing. He was dressed in a classic, light blue suit, with Italian shoes polished to a high gloss.

"Excuse me, sir?" I said.

"Yes?" said the man. He looked surprised when he turned to see who had talked to him.

"I heard you speaking in English and I would like your help," I said.

"Yes, sure," he said.

I introduced myself, as did he, and he said that he came from South Africa. I told him that we had come from Lusaka and that I needed a public phone to contact someone who was supposed to come and pick us up.

From then, he was very helpful. He helped me change the money we had in dollars into Mozambique currency – Mozambican Metical. Then he showed me a shop around the corner where you could make both national and international calls. I tried to call both my uncle and his friend, but once again, no one would pick up. I kept calling – no answer. It didn't even go onto an answering machine.

The South African man was late for his business and he had to go, but before he left, he gave me his number in case we needed more help.

The only hope we had was to meet this friend of my uncle. I didn't know what to do, nor did my siblings. I was the oldest and I was responsible for us. I was almost 20 years old. My brother was almost 16, and my sister 18.

We spent four hours in Maputo with no idea what to do next. I decided to call the South African man who had helped us. I didn't know what to tell him, but I called him and told him that we really needed his help.

About forty minutes later, he met us at the same place. I explained the situation and told him that we were hopeless.

He said, "I'm afraid the road to South Africa is closed because it was damaged by the heavy rain, and there is no other way of getting to Durban these days."

"Oh my God," I said, holding my forehead.

"You guys said you are from Burundi, right?" he asked.

"Yeah."

"I think the better way is for you to go to the refugee camp. There is one here in Maputo, for Burundian and Rwandan refugees, at a place called Masaka 2. You can wait there until the road is repaired, then continue your journey to South Africa."

I had to decide quickly so that the South African guy could go back to his business. He had made a sacrifice to come and help us, so I decided not to waste his time. I agreed to his proposal. After all, we were refugees and we had nothing to lose.

The South African man arranged a taxi to take us to the refugee camp, and we headed to Masaka 2. I sat in the front passenger seat. Annie and Lambert were on the back seat. We were all quiet. The taxi driver only spoke Portuguese.

"What if this guy kidnaps us?" I said to my siblings, speaking in the Kinyarwanda language. We all laughed but kept looking through the windows of the taxi, looking at the city of Maputo.

Half an hour later, we approached the refugee camp, which was clearly signed. The camp looked very different from the one in Tanzania; it was modern and well-built. At least we knew the taxi driver was taking us to the right address.

We paid the taxi driver and got out. As we did, I saw a lady standing outside a big house which looked like a hall. "Excuse me," I said to her. "Do you speak either Kirundi or Kinyarwanda?"

"I speak Kinyarwanda. I'm from Rwanda." *Communication won't be an issue again*, I thought.

The Tsunami

We reported at the reception and we were registered as new refugees in Mozambique. When we filled in the forms, I asked Annie and Lambert if we could add our father's name (Kana) to our first names. They all agreed. From that day we have officially had two first names: Kana Josée Bizimana, Kana Annie Nikiza, and Kana Lambert Matsiko. We were given a place to stay in the camp and tokens for getting our food.

The next day, a tragedy happened in Maputo. It had been raining all over Mozambique. People were dying.

Others had been displaced from their ruined homes. Some of the roads had closed. It was the time of the Tsunami.

We all stayed in our houses because it was very dangerous. The city was full of water, houses were destroyed by rain, cars were submerged and destroyed, people died in great numbers. There was even one woman who gave birth in a tree when she had tried to escape the floods. It was terrible. I didn't know how to swim so I knew it would be the end if I was caught out in the water.

The other problem was that we had to go to the home affairs office in the city centre to register as new refugees in Mozambique. We had a deadline for registration, but the roads were full of water. There was no transport from Masaka to Maputo.

We had only two days remaining, so we walked in water up to our chests. There was a strong current at times which was so powerful it could pull you away and under the water. I was so scared of the water, but I had to do it. My two siblings knew how to swim, so they would at least be able to save themselves. I remember they used to go and swim in Lake Tanganyika when we lived in Congo, but I never joined them. I have always been scared of big lakes and oceans. I regretted not going with them all those years ago.

While we were wading through the water, trying to cross an invisible road, my sister was at my side and my brother walked behind me in case anything happened to me. There were no life-saving guards. Everyone was looking out for his or her own safety.

The water was like a deep river and it started getting rough. I was pushed by a wave and fell into the water.

My brother tried to save me, but he couldn't manage on his own. Finally, a man behind my brother helped him – thanks to God.

We finally got to the home affairs office and registered. But how were we going to get back to the camp? We were going to use the same road again? *Oh my God*, I said silently. *Lord, please help us, please help me, help me, help me.*

Finally, my prayers were answered. There were two men with us. I asked them if I could walk between them so that if anything happened, they could save me. My siblings followed me – they were scared because I had almost drowned a few hours before. From that day, I didn't go anywhere for two months.

Down on my Knees Again

After four months in the refugee camp, the rain started to relent and people returned to their normal business.

I had not informed Father Aloyz about our news. I was sure he was worried about us. My parents did not know we had moved to Mozambique either. So, I went downtown to the public phone and called Father Aloyz. He was not there. The only way I could communicate with my parents was by writing a letter or sending a fax to Arusha where my father was attending the Burundi Peace and Reconciliation. Few people had mobile phones. I was still a student and couldn't afford one. I sent a fax to my father and informed him that we were in Mozambique, and I sent him the address of the camp in case he wanted to contact us. Meanwhile, I kept trying to call Father Aloyz's office for about three weeks, but I couldn't get hold of him.

Life became complicated when we ran out of cash. The money that we had saved for our trip to South Africa was now gone. It was time for me to work out how I was going to get money to help me and my siblings. I had no income. I was used to receiving money from my sponsor in Zambia. In Mozambique, I had no one to help me, and our plan was to continue to South Africa. I had tried to get in touch with my uncle but still I couldn't get him on the phone, nor his friend who lived in Maputo. I asked people if they knew him, but no one seemed to recognize his name.

It was time for Plan B. That has always been my thing; if Plan A fails, then I go for Plan B. That's me to this day. I am an optimist; I always have hope that things will end up in the right way if I work hard or fight for them. I don't easily give up in life.

What's next now? I said to myself.

I couldn't get hold of Father Aloyz or my uncle. I didn't know what had happened to them, so I had to act quickly. It was time, once again, for decisive action. It was now May 2000 and I needed to come up with a solution, either to stay in Mozambique or continue to South Africa and see if we could find our uncle. I knew his address because he had sent me all his details before we left Lusaka.

At that time, I didn't know much about the internet or Google searches, so I had to resort to asking people for information. I came up with the idea of looking for a Jesuit priest to help us. I would tell him we were sponsored by a Jesuit priest in Lusaka and see if that made a difference.

One afternoon, I went to see a guy called John who lived in the camp. I asked him if he knew where any Jesuit priests lived.

"They don't help people anymore," he replied in a very negative tone.

Oh my God, people are desperate, I said to myself, shaking my head.

"I just want to know where they are," I said. "My sponsor back in Zambia is also a Jesuit."

"Oh, okay," John said.

"Even if they don't help people anymore, you never know, I might be lucky," I said.

I was so shocked by John's reactions. This is what I have realized in life, that money can tear people and families apart. We can't do anything without money, but it's also a very dangerous thing. People die because of money, people separate because of money, friends abandon friends because of money, people get jealous of others because of money. Yet, at the same time, we can't live without it. That's how the world is. It's human nature.

I sensed John was getting jealous, thinking I was going to receive a lot of money.

Some days later, I went to this priest named Peter. I explained my situation to him. It was my lucky day. After talking to Father Peter, he went straight to his office and came back with an envelope in his hands. He counted the money for me. It was $500.

"Don't tell other people that I gave you money," he told me.

I fell to my knees and thanked God. I had not been expecting to go back to the camp with such an amount of money! And for sure, I didn't tell anyone apart from my sister and brother. I gave the envelope to my sister and asked her to keep it safe. In the meantime, we heard of a few other priests who were helping refugees. I went to three different priests and managed to get $1,500 in total. This enabled me to start planning the journey to South Africa. The only issue was to know how to get a travel document.

On the Road Again

During that time, I knew a guy who often travelled to South Africa and I was counting on him to help me plan my journey. He told me that he was going to find someone else because he was on his medical break and wasn't allowed to travel long distances. There were a few guys who knew the hidden way to get to Durban, without passing through immigration. Most refugees cross borders without a document, or with a fake one.

I was very impressed when I watched Nelson Mandela's funeral, especially when the Tanzanian president shared how they helped Mandela to cross some borders with a Tanzanian passport. That was one of the things that made me want to start writing this book. I realized that some of the things that had happened to him had happened to us as well.

I wasn't sure how life was going to be in South Africa if I didn't find my uncle. I decided to go on my own and leave my sister and brother in Mozambique. I wanted to go and see what life was like in South Africa. We agreed that if life was manageable there, I would find someone to bring them to South Africa. If the prospects didn't look good, I would return to Mozambique and continue to live there.

One afternoon, the guy who had promised to find someone to take me to South Africa came to see me. He had someone called Peter with him. He told me that Peter was going to South Africa in two days' time, and that he was one of the guys who helped refugees to cross the border to South Africa.

I talked to Peter and we agreed the price ($150) and planned the journey. What came as a surprise was that Peter recognized I was Kana's daughter.

"Yes, I am his firstborn daughter," I said.

"I once came to your place in Uvira-Congo," he said. "But you ignored me. You always showed off and didn't want to talk to people."

I really didn't want to get into a deep conversation with Peter about me showing off and so on, because for me this was a matter of business. The only thing I wanted was to get to South Africa.

The day before I left Mozambique, we had a family meeting with my siblings. I told them that I was going to keep in touch and update them about every move I made, that they were my responsibility and first priority. I asked them to keep praying for me, as I would be praying for them too. I gave them $1,000 and kept the other $500 for the journey. I asked them not to use the money carelessly because it was going to fund their tickets if it was right for them to join me in South Africa.

On 5 June 2000, I travelled to South Africa via Swaziland with Peter.

We took a minibus and set off.

Before we got there, we left the bus and used a path through the bush.

About thirty minutes later, we entered Swaziland.

The Dangerous Forest

Peter and I walked for about twenty minutes to the bus station where we had to take a bus to the South African border. Before we arrived there, Peter asked me if I had money with me.

"I want to keep it on me," he said. "There are a lot of robbers around."

I had paid him the $150 before we left Maputo and had kept $350. I gave him the $350 to keep safe. I would live to regret it.

I was now in Swaziland. Wow! I had learned in History about this country – how they only had kings not presidents. I was really happy to be there.

Later in the afternoon, we took the bus to the South African border. By now I had started to miss my siblings and was wondering what they were doing back in Maputo. I remembered my father's words when I had gone to get my brother from Tanzania. "Wherever you go, don't leave your siblings behind." I started feeling guilty that maybe I had made a bad decision to go ahead without them. But then I kept faith in my hope of finding my uncle in Durban to get my sister and brother over to South Africa.

As we approached the border, it was getting dark and Peter told me that we would not manage to cross the same day. We stopped in the middle of nowhere. There were no houses around, only trees and forest.

I got out of the bus and followed Peter. He said he knew where we were going and showed me a big hill that we were going to climb. The forest was full of dangerous animals and, as we walked in silence, I started seeing lions, leopards and tigers just a few metres away from us. They were sleeping and didn't see us. A few minutes later, I saw the skeletons of people who had been killed by animals in that forest. *Oh my God,* I cried silently. I was so scared I wanted to pee myself. I was crying with fear. I wanted to walk with my eyes closed but I couldn't.

"Don't stress," Peter whispered. "Just keep walking in silence."

We climbed that hill for about forty minutes and finally reached the mountain.

"This is where we have to spend the night," Peter said.

There were few houses there but there was this one man who used to give people who were crossing without a travel document a place to sleep. Obviously, he had to be paid for that. The man offered us a place to sleep, in a small and simple hut. There was no electricity, but he had a big bucket with about fifty litres of water for people to wash their face or brush their teeth. We slept on a mat, but I couldn't close my eyes. I kept asking myself what I was doing on a mountain in the middle of Swaziland. If I closed my eyes and tried to sleep, I would dream of lions coming to kill me! It was a nightmare.

The next day, we had to go and take the bus to continue our journey to South Africa. We walked for about one hour and we reached a village.

Peter pointed ahead.

"South Africa!" he said.

It was just 1 kilometre ahead.

A few minutes later, we had crossed the Swaziland border without passing through immigration.

I had set my feet on South African territory.

Me and Louise, a friend who became a sister.

Me and Yvette, a friend who became a sister.

Me and Liliane, a friend who became a sister.

Chapter 11
THE BATTERED WIFE

When we arrived in Durban, I tried ringing my uncle again but still there was no answer. When we asked people who knew him, they said he was away on business and they didn't know when he was coming back.

I spent that first night at the house of one of Peter's friends.

"Why don't you come to Cape Town?" Peter asked. "It's a nice place."

"Where am I going to live in Cape Town?" I replied. I didn't know anyone there.

"I can give you a place before you figure out what to do next," Peter said.

"How big is your place?"

"It's one bedroom and a living room. I can give my bedroom to you. I will sleep in the living room."

I was uneasy. I suspected he might be lying, but I had no choice.

On 7 June 2000, I spent a whole night and half a day on a clean and luxurious Intercape bus to Cape Town. The countryside was beautiful. I kept looking up to the mountains. Everywhere, the landscape seemed green and lush.

The following afternoon, we arrived. *Oh my God, I am in love with this city,* I cried in my heart.

When I saw Cape Town, it took me back to my childhood when we used to see the tall buildings, well-built roads and smart cars in the books that the missionaries gave us to colour in. The weather was perfect, although cold during the winters (not as cold as European winters though). When we had coloured in those books as children, we used to call it paradise. Now I had found my way to the paradise of Africa. Cape Town had everything you could imagine.

I went to Peter's place at Muizenberg and guess what I found? One room – a studio apartment.

"No way," I said. "Why did you lie to me?"

"That's a man's strength," he answered.

"A man's strength or weakness?" I asked.

He didn't answer, but instead said that he wanted us to go and get something to eat at the nearest 7-Eleven store, so-called because it opened from 7 a.m. to 11 p.m.

Everything was new for me, including good shops that opened until late. Muizenberg was near the beach too, so there was fresh air from the Indian Ocean. All I could say was a silent, *Wow!* It felt like a peaceful place, and I loved it.

Bad News

I asked Peter to give me back the $350 he had kept for me. He returned only $50.

"Where is the rest?"

"Erm…erm, I used it for our tickets to Cape Town."

I was not happy.

I changed the $50 into South African Rand and used some of the money to buy an international phone card to call my sister and brother in Mozambique.

The next day, early in the morning, I went to the public phone which was across the road behind the flat where Peter lived. I called Annie and Lambert.

There was a man from Greece in the refugee camp in Mozambique and he was the only one who had a mobile phone. I had his number in case I wanted to get in touch with my siblings. He gave the phone to them and put me on speaker.

"Hey guys! I've reached South Africa safely and I really like this country."

I told them I couldn't get hold of our uncle and that I had decided to go to Cape Town. I said that I was living at Peter's flat until I could build a new life in Cape Town. Cape Town was the place to be. I wouldn't be returning to Mozambique but would find someone to go and bring them here.

"Send us your address," my sister said. "We have a very important letter from Dad. We received it two days after you had left."

"What's in the letter?" I asked.

"No, I won't tell you," my sister said. She sounded very down. Something wasn't right.

"Are they okay?" I was referring to my parents.

"Yeah, they are okay," my brother replied.

I was running out of credit, so I quickly gave them my address and then the call ended.

A week later, I received a letter from Mozambique. I saw my father's handwriting. I started reading. The first paragraph was a greeting and him asking if we had managed to go back to school. That was always his concern. Then came the second paragraph.

"Guys, you have to be strong for this bad news, but that's how God wanted it to happen."

Before I continued reading, my heart was filled with fear.

Dad went on to share how his last-born child, Deo, had passed away in January the same year. He was only 9 years old.

I didn't finish the letter. I burst into tears. I cried and cried, wishing I was with my siblings so that we could cry together. I was devastated. I felt like the world had caved in on me.

I remembered when I went back to Tanzania in September 1999, how my parents told me that they didn't want to give me both my brothers to take to Zambia, how they didn't want to stay alone. Now, my brother was gone. He was like a son to me. He was born when I was 11 years old and I took care of him, I loved him, and he loved me too. I remember once when he told my mother that she wasn't his mum, that I was his mother.

I was devastated, and I was scared – scared that something might happen to my siblings in Mozambique. I spent the whole month fed up with life. I had this pain in my heart that no one could heal.

Finding Comfort in the Wrong Place

I was still living in Peter's studio flat. He tried to be there for me. He was the only person I knew in Cape Town and he was the only one who knew about my loss.

Living with a guy in the same studio bedroom and having a hard time of course led me into temptation, especially when Peter showed that he was there to comfort me.

The inevitable happened.

I slept with him.

I regretted what I had done. I felt stupid, but it happened and there was nothing I could do could change it.

I tried to hold things together. I went to register at home affairs as a refugee. On my file I included the names of my sister and brother. I said that I was responsible for them.

I also began to find out how I could go back to school, how I could get a part-time job while being at school because I wanted to have my own place.

Sometime towards the end of July, I started feeling sick. I was weak and always sleepy, but I didn't know what was going on. I also felt a lot of pain when I went to pee. I was scared.

I went to the surgery. I explained how I was feeling and they took my blood and asked for some of my urine too. An hour-and-a-half later, the doctor came and told me that my tests showed that I was pregnant.

When I heard the word 'pregnant', I almost fell down. The nurse came and held me from behind, keeping me upright.

I didn't know what to do. I was in shock. I had always dreamed of having kids, but I wanted it to happen at the right time and with the right man.

I asked the doctor if he was sure and he said he was. He also asked me to wait two days for more blood test results.

I didn't say a word to Peter that day.

Two days later, I went back to the hospital and the results showed that I was pregnant. There was no doubt.

When I got home, I told Peter.

"Pregnant? With who?" he asked.

"With you! Who else?"

"How many months pregnant are you?" Peter asked, adding, "Because I don't know who the father is, and I don't think I am responsible."

I had never slept with another man. I had been too busy travelling and I had many responsibilities.

"It's definitely you, Peter."

I really needed to cool down, so I went to the beach. I sat on a bench facing the ocean. I felt confused and lost.

How was I going to cope? What was life going to look like? How was I going to complete my studies at college? What would I say to my siblings? I saw people walking along the beach, laughing, and looking happy. I started asking God if those people were luckier than me. I was totally disoriented.

Later in the evening, I went back home, but I didn't want to talk to Peter. I just wanted time to myself. After all, he had said that he wasn't the father and that he was not responsible.

Training for the Future

One day I went downtown because I wanted some fresh air in one of the parks I had seen in the city. Before I went there, I sat and read every page of the magazine I had bought. While I was reading, a man approached me. He started talking to me. Sometimes I ignored people, but this time I didn't. He asked me what my name was and where I came from. I told him.

"Wow! My name is Didier and I am from Rwanda too!"

"Nice to meet you Didier," I said.

I told him that I was new in Cape Town and that I was looking for a job. He said that he could get me a job in a hotel as a receptionist, but he also advised me to do a short training course in hotel reception. I was impressed; Didier was telling me what I wanted to hear. He even told me that, if I was interested, he would show me where to get a form and fill it in straight away.

"The course starts two weeks today," he said. "And the good news is that refugees don't have to pay for the training."

"Sure!" I said. "I'm free and we can go now."

We walked to the other side of Cape Town. As we went up the elevator and walked down a corridor, Didier asked me if I was single. I said yes, but that I was waiting to be a mum soon. He looked surprised.

"Are you pregnant?"

"Yeah, I just found out few days ago."

"Who is the father? You said you were single."

"It's a long and complicated story. I don't want to talk about it right now. Let's just concentrate on what we have come to do."

We found the forms and I filled them in. The secretary made a copy of the temporary document I had received from the home affairs office and they told me to wait for an answer to when I could start the course.

I thanked Didier and told him that I was going to stay in touch with him after I had sorted everything out. I told him I was still dealing with a lot of stressful situations, but that I would call him soon.

He gave me his mobile number and we said goodbye. I decided to keep my baby, believing it was God's plan, and I don't regret that decision.

When I returned, I told Peter about Didier and about the training course. He reacted like a lion in the jungle.

"You said you are pregnant with my child? That means now you are now my girlfriend."

"Girlfriend?" I cried.

Even if I was pregnant with his child, part of me was adamant – I wasn't dating him. But another part of my heart said, *Maybe I should try to get to know this guy and give my baby the chance to know their father.*

A week later, I received a letter from the college which said that I had been offered a place to do the training.

That same week, I went back to the doctor for the check-up and the dates for my regular pregnancy check-ups at Somerset Hospital. I didn't expect to receive any help from Peter and that's why I wanted to do the course so that I could get a job and feed my baby. Meanwhile, I was also planning how my siblings could get to Cape Town.

Money, Money, Money

I don't know who told my father that I had left my sister and brother in Mozambique, but one day I went to the public phone to call my father because I needed some money. I wanted to ask him for $200 so that I could get the ticket to take me to college and buy a cheap mobile phone. While I was talking to him, he asked me if I was with Annie and Lambert so that he could talk to them. I lied and told him that they had stayed at home. "I need to talk to them. Next time you should put them on the phone," he said.

Oh my God, I said silently.

The next day I went to collect the money my father had sent to me via Western Union. I bought a small Motorola cell phone. It was my first phone.

It was already the middle of August and I was starting to suffer from morning sickness. Some weeks later, I began college. I was doing something that I would enjoy doing as a job. I liked that.

I told Peter that if he wanted me to be his girlfriend, he needed to know that I had a big responsibility given by my father to look after my two siblings. If he wanted to continue living with me, my sister and brother must be allowed to come and join me. I made it very clear, adding that I was looking for someone to get them to Cape Town.

"Who?" Peter shouted.

"Someone in Mozambique," I replied.

Before I said another word, he raised his hand and hit me in the face.

Shouting, he said, "I told you that child you are carrying is not mine. You should tell me who the father is."

He hit me again and again. I screamed so loudly that the man who looked after the flat – the concierge – knocked on the door.

"What's going on?" he asked Peter.

"It's my girlfriend. She is crying because she is in pain."

"No!" I cried. "He is lying! He just hit me for no reason!"

From that time, I lived an abusive life in which domestic violence became my 'normal'.

A week later, I called a guy from Mozambique and asked him if he could do me a favour and bring my sister and brother to South Africa. I told him that he shouldn't worry about their transport money or his. I had left $1,000 with my siblings, so there was nothing to worry about. He agreed and told me that he was going to do it at the end of September.

One day after college, I had to go to the hospital for my check-up. On my way back home, I used a shortcut. I hesitated at first to use it because it had started getting dark, but then I pushed my concerns aside and went. Two men wearing masks attacked me, both holding knives. They told me to give them money. I started panicking and told them that I didn't have any.

"Give us some money. We know your father is getting a lot of money in Arusha."

I started crying and shaking.

But how lucky I was. A man appeared in that same shortcut and the two men disappeared.

I ran towards him and told him what had happened.

"This is a dangerous area to use at night, especially for a young lady like you," he said. He helped me to get home safely, escorting me the whole way.

When I got home, I told Peter what had happened and that I wanted to live somewhere else. Though I was still angry at him beating me for no reason, I didn't have any other choice but to stay with him until I finished my training and got a job.

Refugee Protection

I always say that no matter what circumstances we face in life, everything happens for a reason.

I kept asking myself, who those guys were who talked about the money that my father was getting from

Arusha. I was confused. Then I remembered how I had gone twice to collect the money from my father. But he had sent it while he was in Dar es Salaam, not in Arusha. I knew that my father was participating in Burundi peace negotiations in Arusha. Was this going to put my life in danger?

One day I went to home affairs to get my refugee status ID card and I talked to one of the officers about what happened when two men attacked me. That officer told me that this was a very important matter and that I had to report it to the UNHCR (United Nations High Commission for Refugees) and get refugee protection.

The next day after college, I went to the UNHCR and asked to talk to someone about refugee protection. A few minutes later, someone from social services came and had a chat with me. They asked me if I had proof that my father was attending the Burundi peace negotiations. I said yes. They gave me forms for resettlement on the grounds of refugee protection. I took them home and completed them, asking Peter if I could put his name under where it said 'partner'. I thought I was doing the right thing for my baby. He pretended not to have heard what I had asked him. Then, a minute later, he reacted.

"Let me have a look at those forms. You should tick married. Otherwise they won't accept that we are partners."

"But we are not married!"

"Just listen to what I am telling you" Peter shouted.

"But I don't want to lie!"

He raised his hand and hit me in my face. He threatened to burn the form with a lighter. I screamed and told him that I would write what he had told me to write. The next day, Peter came home with a wedding ring. He said I had to wear it every day so that people thought that I was a married woman. If he ever saw me not wearing it, he would beat me to death.

I became very miserable after that. I didn't know what to do. I filled in the forms. I also included details of my sister and brother.

I took the forms back and the official told me to return after two weeks, adding that I needed to come back with my partner and my brother and sister because I had put all their details as people who lived with me.

Two weeks!

I made a quick call to the guy who was going to bring my siblings and I promised to pay him extra if he could do it sooner. He didn't hesitate. I immediately called Annie and Lambert in Mozambique and asked them to get ready. By this time, Peter and I had moved to a new place called Kensington.

At the new place in Kensington, there was one lady with five children – all boys. She was called Claudine. I went to introduce myself to her and told her that I was her new neighbour. From that day, something clicked between us and she became like my mother and I became like her daughter. Everyone called her Auntie Claudine.

I started praying to God, asking him to look after my siblings on their journey to South Africa. I remembered the forest with the wild animals in Swaziland.

Congrats Sis!

Three days later, Annie and Lambert arrived in Durban. It was the end of August. My sister was sick and I didn't want to let them travel to Cape Town from Durban on their own. The guy who brought them down to Durban wasn't coming to Cape Town, so I decided to fetch them. On the bus journey, I couldn't sleep because I was nervous about how I was going to tell them that I was pregnant.

When I saw my siblings, I felt relieved and I couldn't wait to make a phone call to my parents. I had stopped calling my father until my brother and sister had come to South Africa. We first talked to my mother, then later to my father. My parents were happy to hear that we were all together.

I was almost three months pregnant now and was wearing big T-shirts to hide my belly. I have always been a skinny girl, but I had started gaining a bit of weight. I was scared that my brother or my sister would find out before I told them I was pregnant.

After one day in Durban, I asked them if we could go down to the beach and sit in one of the restaurants. "We can have a nice meal together and catch up on some news."

When we arrived, we all had Coke to drink. My brother and I had fish, salad and chips. My sister had the same, except she changed the fish for a steak.

We chatted about everything. I told them how the two guys attacked me and that I had reported it to the UNHCR for refugee protection. I told them that I had an appointment in a week's time, and they needed to come with me. Still, I didn't know how to tell them that I was pregnant.

"Erm... guys," I started saying, but then stopped and took a deep breath.

"What?" my brother asked.

"I want to tell you something. But I only want your support, that's all."

They both looked curious.

"I am pregnant."

"Is it Peter?" my brother asked.

"Yeah."

"Congrats sis!" They both shouted, hugging me.

I burst into tears of joy.

The next morning, we went to book our coach tickets and we left the same afternoon for Cape Town. "Wow!" I heard my brother saying. "Sis! See how cool this is! Look at the chimpanzees!" My sister was enjoying a nap. It was her first time in a lux coach.

We reached Cape Town the next day around 1 p.m. I asked my siblings if we could do a bit of a tour. I wanted to show them the parts of the city I had already visited. My sister was speechless when she saw how beautiful Cape Town was. My brother kept saying, "Wow!" They both loved Cape Town and I was relieved to see them happy.

We took a bus and went home to Kensington. Before we entered the house, I introduced Annie and Lambert to Auntie Claudine. "This is our second mum," I said. We all loved her and to this day we are still in touch. Auntie Claudine and my mother are the women that I love most in my life.

Auntie Claudine

The day after my sister and brother arrived in Cape Town, I took them to the home affairs office to get registered. They issued the temporary document to use before my siblings received their refugee status.

Three days later, after a pleasant weekend at the beach, we went around the city and looked in the shopping malls with Auntie Claudine. Then, on Monday, we all went to the UNHCR for our appointment.

We arrived at the reception and a few minutes later a lady came to shake our hands. She asked us to follow her into her office. There were two other men sitting there, waiting to talk to us.

They interviewed us and then said they were going to do an investigation and check if my father was really participating in the Burundi peace negotiations in Arusha. They would call me and make another appointment to see us again.

I was about to finish my hotel reception training and I had registered to do another course on mediation and counselling.

The days went by and my belly was growing. It was October and I was five months pregnant. I still had not told my parents. I was enduring abuse from Peter and I wasn't enjoying my pregnancy. I had not even bought one item of clothing for my baby. I didn't know where to find money. I was suffering in silence.

One day I asked Peter to give me some money to buy some baby stuff. He gave me only 250 Rand, which is about £15. He woke up every day saying that he was going to work, even though I didn't know what kind of a job he did. Peter would give me rules and tell me what to do. He would say that he was the one who was feeding me and my siblings, that I had to follow his rules.

One day I was sitting outside and looking hopeless and Auntie Claudine came to talk to me. She had seen me washing Peter's clothes by hand and ironing them. She had suspected something wasn't right in my relationship. She wanted to talk to me as a mother. She asked me if I was okay, then got straight to the point and said that I shouldn't lie to her, that she could see I wasn't happy.

That day, I told Auntie Claudine the whole story about how I had met Peter and how he started abusing me when I was four weeks pregnant. She really felt sad to see me suffering when I was supposed to be enjoying my pregnancy.

"I'm afraid that Peter will beat me if I don't do what he orders me to do."

"Don't worry. From now on, you will be using my washing machine to wash Peter's clothes. We will make sure he doesn't find out about it. Peter wants to treat you as if you are his housekeeper, but I won't allow that to happen to you. If Peter hits you again, we will report it to social services."

I had never heard about social services before. In some parts of Africa, women live a miserable life of being beaten or hit by their partners and they don't have anywhere to report about their abusive life. Others keep it a secret because they depend on their partner's income or because they consider it shameful for a woman to leave her partner and divorce him. So most of the time, women in that situation live an unhappy life, with a big risk of been killed or ending up with a disability. A lot of men take advantage of that and treat their partners without dignity and respect.

That's how Peter treated me.

By the time my pregnancy reached six months, I had not bought anything for my baby. I had no money and Peter never wanted to give me any for baby stuff. I had no idea what to do.

I asked Auntie Claudine if she could sew some clothes for my baby; she had a sewing machine. When

I explained that Peter only gave me 250 Rand to buy baby stuff, she was appalled.

"Are you joking? Do you really mean 250 Rand?"

I nodded.

"Do you know the gender of the baby?" she asked.

"No. I want it to be a surprise."

"Don't worry. I will make some baby clothes for you," she said.

Coming to America

At the beginning of November, someone called me from the main office of UNHCR.

"Can I talk to Miss Josée, please?"

"Speaking."

"Will you be able to come to the office tomorrow around 2 p.m. for another interview, please? And we need all of you again."

"Sure. No problem. I will tell the others."

The next day, my sister, my brother, Peter, and I went to the UNHCR office. The secretary introduced herself as Patricia, but they called her Patty.

About ten minutes later, I saw a lady walking down the corridor holding our file. She was coming to talk to us.

"My name is Lee Anne". She introduced herself.

We shook hands and we all went into her office. The two men from our first interview were there again. One of them said that they had done their research and found a picture in one of the latest newspapers showing someone they said might be my father. When I looked at the photo, it was a picture of my father greeting President Nelson Mandela.

"Congratulations guys. You have passed your interview and you are going to live in Virginia in America. We are resettling you. We wanted proof that you are Kana's children, and you have just provided it. We will consider you political refugees as from now."

At first, I thought I was dreaming. When I went to report about being attacked by strangers, I thought they might relocate us to another side of Cape Town for our safety. But now I was hearing America! I was over the moon.

None of us reacted. It was beyond our wildest imaginations.

"Okay," Lee Anne said. "I will send the fax to our main office for refugees in Pretoria. We will get back to you soon and tell you the departing date. It will probably take three more months until everything gets sorted."

I thanked everyone there, and then we went back home, still not believing what we had just heard.

"Guys, soon we will be flying," I told my siblings.

"I still can't believe it," my sister said.

"Me either," my brother added.

Meanwhile, Peter didn't say a word. He looked like someone who had another plan in his head.

A Father's Blessing

We went back home. I wanted to tell Auntie Claudine, but I decided to wait until they told us the date we would be leaving.

I told Annie and Lambert that I thought it was time for me to tell our parents that I was pregnant. We wouldn't tell them about the America story. I wanted to keep it a surprise.

One week later, I felt strong enough to call my parents. I bought enough credits and held the phone in my hand for about an hour. Whenever I tried to call, I felt scared. Finally, I took a deep breath. As always, it was my father who picked up.

"Have you started school already?" he asked. He knew that I was on a training course, but he wanted me to go to a proper college for a good career.

"I have something to tell you," I said. "But I first need your forgiveness and blessing."

"What did you do?" my father asked.

"I am pregnant."

"Okay. How many months?" my father asked me, without surprise or anger.

My sister and brother were standing beside me.

My sister whispered in my ears, "Tell him that you are already six months."

I did.

I will never forget how my father congratulated me, saying that he was going to be a grandpa. Then he handed the phone to my mother so that I could tell her too. Now my heart was really racing. My mother was stricter than my father.

"Tell me, what's new?" she asked.

"I just told papa that I am pregnant."

Silence. I really wanted to drop the phone, but I resisted. The only thing that worried my mother was that she wanted to be there for me. I assured her that I was okay and told her about Auntie Claudine.

My father took the phone back. He wanted to know who the father was. I tried to explain but not in full detail. I said I would tell him more when I called them again.

We never spoke about it again. It was done. They had blessed me. Now, all I had to do was wait for the baby to be born and then surprise them with the news that we had gone to America.

Miracles from Heaven

Cape Town was treating us well. We had Auntie Claudine – who was born there – and she knew every corner of the city. I had completed my training as a hotel receptionist and had now started going once a week for an eight-week course on mediation and counselling.

Christmas 2000 was the best ever for me and my siblings. It was our first Christmas in South Africa. Everything was magical – all around there were Christmas lights, Christmas songs, Christmas decorations – things I had only seen and heard in the movies. It was crazy. We enjoyed life to the full. We spent our Christmas on the beach in Muizenberg, eating a Christmas picnic.

By January 2001, I was seven months pregnant. One afternoon, I was heading for my check-up at the hospital, when I heard my phone ringing. It was Lee Anne from the UNHCR asking if I could go to the office the next day. This time I was to go for an interview, but I asked Annie and Lambert to come with me, just to keep me company.

When we arrived, Patty and Lee Anne were both very happy to see us. I didn't understand why. We went to sit in Lee Anne's office. Patty joined us and we all had something to drink. They wanted to let us know that they had received a response from the main office of refugees in Geneva and that our resettlement was approved. But there was a big issue: I couldn't do a long-haul flight so late in my pregnancy. We were supposed to leave Cape Town at the end of February 2001, but my baby was due at the end of March. We would have to wait until I gave birth.

The UNHCR was very concerned about our safety in Cape Town, so they decided to move us to Pretoria. Peter and my brother moved first, and my sister and I stayed in Cape Town until I gave birth. They had arranged a place for us to stay at the Commodore Hotel, near the hospital where I was going to give birth. The plan was to go to Pretoria three weeks after that.

Miracles were falling from heaven. I really couldn't believe how quickly things were moving.

We went back home, and I told Peter what they had decided. He reacted weirdly, but I didn't care.

Auntie Claudine was my neighbour, so this time I had to tell her. I asked if we could take a walk around Kensington. I told her that we were leaving soon.

"Where are you moving to?"

"We are preparing to go to America, but before we leave Cape Town, we need to be in Pretoria. But for me and my sister we will be staying in Cape Town until the baby comes."

At first, she was relieved to hear that she was going to see my baby before I left, but then she was sad at the thought that we were leaving her. We had made a very good team; she was like our mother and we were like her children. Yet, like a good mum, she was also happy for us.

Three days before we moved, we gave most of our stuff we had to Auntie Claudine. Peter sold other items. I asked him to give me some money from the sales to buy stuff for the baby. He refused. I prayed every day, asking God to help me. I put everything in his hands, because I didn't know where to find money to buy things for my baby. I was waiting for more miracles to happen, like all the others that were popping up from nowhere.

When Thank You is not Enough

Peter and my brother went to Pretoria. Everything was arranged by UNHCR for their accommodation. My sister and I stayed in the hotel. It was a four-star hotel. We were given breakfast, lunch and dinner. There was a swimming pool. The rooms were chic and very clean. I enjoyed it!

One day, Patty and Lee Anne invited me and my sister for lunch at UCT (The University of Cape Town). Before we went to meet them, my sister came up with an idea. "Maybe you should tell Lee Anne and Patty that you don't have anything for your baby."

I considered it.

While we ate lunch in the restaurant, I did what my sister suggested.

"No way!" Lee Anne said. "Why didn't you tell me before? We could have arranged something for you."

"We should do something," Patty said. "Just give us few days and we will get back to you."

"Thanks," I said, tears falling down my face.

A week later, at the end of February, Lee Anne called and told me that her and Patty had something for the baby. The same afternoon, my sister and I went to see them. I will never, ever, ever forget that day. They gave me two big suitcases full of baby clothes, feeding bottles, everything that I needed for the baby. I still have one of the suitcases to this day. Since they didn't know the baby's gender, all the clothes were unisex.

Miracles again, I said in my heart.

My sister was also speechless. It had been her idea, so I thanked her a lot for that. That was one of the many gestures of support from my siblings. I needed them to be there for me, and they always have.

To say thank you to these two lovely women wasn't enough. I didn't know what to say or where to start. The only thing I said was, "May God protect you and give you a long life to live. You didn't save my life, but you have saved my baby's life. Thank you a million."

That was all I could think of saying.

Lee Anne hugged me and reassured me that everything was going to be okay. Patty gave me a lovely hug too before Lee Anne drove us back to the hotel. On the way, the first thing I did was call Pretoria to talk to my brother and tell him what had happened. Peter didn't come first in my mind. He acted as if he wasn't involved at all in the life of my child.

While Lee Anne drove us, we stopped at the traffic lights.

"Have you chosen a name for your baby?" Lee Anne asked.

That was a good question. I had not yet thought about it I had been so stressed.

"If it's a girl," I said. "I'll call her Lee Ann. If it's a boy, I don't know. Maybe Lee Patrick. The Lee from Lee Anne, and Patrick from Patty."

She was so excited to hear that. "I will pray for your baby to be a girl," she said.

We arrived at the hotel where my sister looked at each of the clothes, arranged them to take to the hospital. She washed and ironed them, then packed them in the suitcase.

We remained in a state of readiness.

The baby was due on 30 March 2001.

A Wonderful Surprise

15 March was my twenty-first birthday. The day before my birthday Lee Anne called and asked me if we could go for lunch somewhere around town and I accepted.

"I will pick you up tomorrow morning at half past eleven," she said.

The next day at 11:30 a.m., Lee Anne's car was parked out the front of the hotel. My sister and I got in the car, and Lee Anne drove us to UCT. I found it weird because the day before, Lee Anne had said we would be having lunch in town." I didn't know what she was up to.

When we arrived, she asked me to stay in the car, and asked my sister to go with her to the office. She said she wanted my sister's help lifting some boxes. Ten minutes later, my sister came out of the UCT building and asked me to go with her so that I could have a drink before we went for lunch. I got out of the car, entered the UCT building using the main entrance, walked down the corridor, following in my sister's steps. As we entered one of the meeting rooms, I saw about ten ladies, including Lee Anne and Patty.

"Surprise!" They all shouted.

"Oh my God!" I cried.

I didn't know what to say. I just looked at my sister. "So, you knew all this?"

"Yeah, I knew everything from the beginning."

"Cut your cake! Cut your cake! Cut your cake!" everyone shouted.

I was shaking. I was over the moon. I felt the love from everyone in that room. I was so happy.

I blew out the twenty-one candles on my lovely chocolate birthday cake, cut it in pieces, and served everyone in the room.

I felt like my brother was missing out, so I took my phone, went outside and called him in Pretoria.

"Hey bro! You have no idea what is happening down here!"

"Tell me, sis...."

"They just surprised me on my birthday!" I said.

"Oh shit!" he cried. "By the way, happy birthday sis!"

"So, you forgot, huh? Anyway, thanks!" I said.

I hung up before my brother asked me if I wanted to talk to Peter. He knew well enough that things were not going well between us. I then returned to the meeting room to have lunch before some of the ladies had to go back to their classes.

My Daughter's Birth

Two days later, on the morning of Saturday 17th, I woke up with a hunger that I had never felt before. I went to the toilet and when I wiped myself, I saw some blood on the toilet tissue.

"Oh my God, I screamed, walking to the bedroom where my sister was still enjoying her morning nap.

"Sis! I think the day has come! I just saw blood!"

My sister looked scared. Then she said, "Let me check the suitcase and see if everything is ready. Take a shower and then we will go to the hospital."

The hospital was just few minutes' walk from the hotel. We arrived, and my sister stayed in the waiting room. When they had finished checking how soon the baby would be born, they decided to keep me at the hospital.

Late in the evening, I started having some real contractions. The pain lasted the whole night.

The next day, 18 March, was the day my little brother Deo had been born. I was praying that God would let my baby come the same day, so that I could always remember him on my baby's birthday.

I kept having pain after pain. I was holding my Bible all the time and praying. Two days in pain, but the baby wasn't coming.

Monday the 19th, the midwife came to check how far I was. She found me in so much pain. I prayed, "Lord, I thought I was going to have my baby yesterday on Deo's birthday. Please let my baby come today, on Lambert's birthday. At least my baby will have the same birth date as one of my brothers."

After the midwife was done checking, she decided to take me into the delivery room and they broke the water. It was around 10 a.m. Before they took me there, I asked them to call my sister and tell her to come to the hospital.

I had more pain for just under two hours.

At 11:45 a.m., I gave birth to a beautiful girl.

I was the happiest girl on earth at that moment. I felt so much love when they put my baby on my chest. My sister was so happy, she kept laughing.

"Did you call Lee Anne?" I asked my sister.

"Yes, I think she is outside waiting for us."

I am sure Lee Anne was keen to know if I had given birth to a girl, knowing that I was going to name my baby after her.

When we walked out from the delivery room, I sat in a wheelchair and my sister pushed. As we went towards the restroom, Lee Anne was sitting in the waiting room. When she saw me, she came running and hugged me.

"Tell me it's a girl!" she said.

"Yeah, it's a little you," I said.

And I named my baby Lee Ann after the one who had helped me so much. The only difference was that I removed the last 'e'. I was so happy that my baby had the same date of birth as my brother Lambert.

Saying Sad Goodbyes

That afternoon, the midwife finished checking me and the baby. Everything looked good and they released me to go home.

Lee Anne drove us back to the hotel where we had to wait two weeks before we could go to Pretoria to join my brother and Peter. I called Peter to let him know that the baby was doing great. On the phone he seemed happy. I started thinking that maybe his daughter was going to make him realize that he had to change and be a better man. I was wrong.

The first day with baby Lee Ann was magical. She slept between me and my sister on the same bed. My sister would say, "Today, the baby will face me for two hours." I would say, "She will face me for the other three hours." She was so beautiful. She didn't cry at all. She was simply an amazing princess.

The next day, Auntie Claudine called to tell me that she was on her way to the hotel to see the baby. She knocked on the door and my sister went to open it. "Congratulations!" Auntie Claudine said. She looked happy and excited as she pulled a big suitcase into the room while I sat on the bed feeding my baby. I didn't know what was in that suitcase. As it turned out, it was full of my baby's clothes.

Oh my God, I said in my heart. Auntie Claudine had taken my breath away. I had asked her to sew some baby clothes for me. What I didn't know was that she was waiting to know the gender of the baby so that she could surprise me. I was so emotional.

Auntie Claudine took my mother's role, showing me how to bathe the baby. She taught me everything about how to recognize and interpret my baby's signs and reactions.

Five days after I had given birth, Lee Anne called me and told me that the plan of going to America had changed. The other group that we were supposed to go with had already left a month before, and the UNHCR had planned to take the next group to USA after nine months. The main office for refugees in Geneva had therefore decided to resettle us in one of the European countries. And that country was the Netherlands.

When my baby was three weeks old, we were ready to leave Cape Town and head to Pretoria. The day before we left, Lee Anne and Patty came to say goodbye to me and my sister. Lee Anne had booked the coach for us for our journey the next day, and she had booked the taxi to take us to the coach station. This time, the coach was more comfortable.

Lee Anne and Patty gave us gifts. Lee Anne offered a Bible to little baby Lee Ann. That was the gift that I had always wanted my baby to have. It was beautiful – a sign of protection and a source of blessing for her life on this earth.

On the morning of 6 April 2001, Auntie Claudine arrived to escort us to the coach station. That day was emotional. We all hugged and cried.

The coach left at 2 p.m. for Pretoria.

As we travelled, I was asking myself what Peter's reaction would be when he saw his daughter. I wasn't expecting him to be excited, though I hoped he would be. He had caused me pain and mistreated me during my pregnancy, so I wasn't really expecting miracles from him. I knew that my brother was going to be the happiest boy on earth; he shared the same birthday as his niece, so he had good reason.

We spent all night on the coach and the next day around 11 a.m., we reached Pretoria. My brother and Peter had come to wait for us at the coach station. My brother was so happy to see his two big sisters and his little niece. Peter also looked happy, which surprised me, but I didn't interpret it as a big deal.

The UNHCR had arranged for our accommodation in one of the flats outside the city of Pretoria.

I shared a room with Peter and my siblings shared another room in the same building.

Domestic Violence

One afternoon a week later, Peter came home and started smoking in the room where the baby was sleeping. I had never seen him smoking before. It wasn't even a normal cigarette smell. I thought it smelt like drugs.

I became angry that he didn't realize that there was a baby of three weeks in the room, and that she could inhale the smoke. When I asked him to go and do it outside, he yelled at me: "You don't tell me what to do!"

"But there is a baby here. Can't you see? A 3-week-old baby, for God's sake!"

"I told you not to tell me what to do, so just shut up!"

"Don't tell me to shut up when I am trying to protect my baby."

Peter took a breakable, two-litre bottle and started beating my back. "Women shouldn't give me instructions on what to do. I am a man and you should respect that." He kept hitting me while he was yelling. I had only just given birth and still had not yet recovered. I was still in pain – even more so now that I was being abused. To this day I still have back pains, and my daughter still can't stand the smell of a cigarette.

I cried, and my baby cried. I took her in my arms, and when I breastfed her, my tears were dropping on my baby's face. I was so hurt.

"This has to end," I told Peter.

"We will see who's the man, me or you!" Peter shouted. "Remember the papers! We are officially married." Suddenly, I felt so stupid that I had ticked the box where it said 'married' when I was filling in the resettlement forms. We were still waiting for the Netherlands to send us the travel documents, so it was too late for me to come out of that relationship.

An hour later, I took my baby and went to my siblings' room. I wanted to cool down. I felt like a volcano had erupted all over me. I was sweating as if I had been in a sauna, and I was shaking like a small house in a big earthquake.

I didn't even know what to say to my brother and sister. I only asked my sister to help me to take care of the baby, that I wanted to have some rest and get some sleep.

I had never dated Peter. I didn't love him. What happened between us to cause me to end up in bed with him was something that could happen to anyone. And when I put his name down as my partner while filling in the resettlement forms, I did it because I wanted to give the relationship a chance. Surely it was going to be better for my child to grow up with her father. I was wrong, and I regretted it all, including giving my daughter his surname. At the same time, I did what I always did. I told myself, *It's okay Josée. Everything is gonna be fine. Just keep fighting and believing that God can help you pass through that pain.* I had no choice but to encourage myself.

No Longer Just a Dream

Two days before we left South Africa for the Netherlands, we went shopping. By that time, I had spent almost a month-and-half without talking to Peter. I had stayed in my siblings' room right up until the day we left South Africa.

As we went around the biggest shopping mall in Pretoria, Peter tried to apologize, saying that he was sorry for beating me. I simply told him that it wasn't the right time. I was very hurt and just wanted to get ready for our journey to Europe.

On 15 May 2001, at about 4 p.m., a guy called Richard from UNHCR was waiting outside the building to drive us to Johannesburg's O.R Tambo International Airport. Our flight was at 8 p.m. and we were flying with KLM.

"Are you ready, guys?" he asked.

"Yeah, I guess we are," I replied.

"Tomorrow you will not be African any longer. We will be calling you European," he said, while putting our luggage in the boot of the car.

It took a while for us to get to the airport because it was the end of the working day and everyone was going home. The highway was full of traffic.

It was the first time that any of us had been on an airplane journey. We all looked nervous.

When we arrived at the airport, Richard presented our travel documents from the Netherlands. Each of us had a light blue 'One Way Passport' – passports they give to people being resettled in the Netherlands. Each of us had one, even baby Lee Ann.

Richard took them to the check-in desk. My brother and Peter followed him with our luggage. Richard was handed our boarding passes.

"Guys!" he said. "This is it. You have two hours before your departure. Go through immigration and then follow the signs to your gate. Wait there for boarding."

We had no idea what that meant. It was all new to us.

Before we went through immigration, I phoned Lee Anne, Patty and Auntie Claudine, and told them that we were finally flying. They were all happy for us and each one of them wished us a safe journey and asked me to keep in touch with them.

"For sure!" I said.

I thought about my parents in Dar es salaam, Tanzania. They didn't know about us going to Europe. I remembered my father telling me to try get to South Africa or Europe for a better life and a good education. I wondered why he entrusted me with the responsibility of taking care of my two siblings when I was still so young. We had managed to get ourselves to South Africa which was still in Africa, but to get to Europe or America wasn't one of my plans. I had not even thought that, one day, it could happen for us. Cape Town had been Europe for us.

But then I realized how lucky my family was, how God can answer your prayers and make your dreams come true. I realized that my father's wishes and dreams were being fulfilled and I also realized how blessed I was to have my firstborn little girl and my two siblings with me.

Richard said goodbye and told us he would visit us when he came to the Netherlands. He wished us good luck in our new life, as well as a safe journey.

We all passed through immigration, went through the security area, and followed the signs to the gates where we had to wait before we boarded. While waiting, I sat and said a silent prayer, thanking God for everything he had done for us. I asked God to give me strength to deal with the situation between me and Peter, and finally I asked him to bless our journey.

Two hours later, the plane started moving.

It was no longer a dream.

It was real.

It was the most wonderful feeling I ever had.

My baby slept all night, until 6 a.m.

Just two hours before we landed in Amsterdam, we were given our breakfast at about 7 a.m. I changed my baby's diaper and breastfed her. We received a nice postcard from KLM and then we heard the pilot welcoming everyone to Amsterdam at around 8:20 a.m., on the morning of 16 May 2001.

We had landed at Schiphol Airport, Amsterdam.

We were on European soil.

From the left is auntie Claudine, I am in the middle and auntie Claudine's sons.

Me and my kids, Lee Ann and Lenny in Berlin – Germany.
(Summer 2010)

Chapter 12
THE WORST AND BEST OF MEN

"Welcome to the Netherlands," the immigration officer said as we handed in our one-way Dutch passports.

We retrieved our luggage, then followed the exit signs until we found an official from immigration holding a board with our names. He welcomed us in good English. Later, I learned that most people in the Netherlands speak English.

After a brief wait, accompanied by tea and biscuits, another official spoke to us in one of the offices inside the airport.

"Welcome to Holland, the country of freedom and peace. Let's check if your names and other details are correct, because these will be the details which are going to be officially registered for you in the Netherlands."

We all went through the forms and corrected some spelling mistakes and altered a few other details. At the place where it was written that I was married to Peter, I was not happy. I wanted so much to change it, but then decided against it. Maybe my relationship with Peter would work out. Again, I was thinking about my baby.

Two hours later, after the interview, we were transported by taxi to a refugee centre at Culemborg. As we passed through the centre of Amsterdam, I looked through the window, trying to study the town and see if there was anything new and attractive. Having come from Cape Town, I realized that I had seen it all.

An hour later, when we reached Culemborg, I saw cows grazing in a huge field surrounded by a lot of water. "Oh my God!" I said to my siblings. "So many cows, just like in Africa!"

My brother said, "Remember, most of the farmers in Europe live in the Netherlands, Sis, and in Holland there is water everywhere."

When we arrived at the refugee centre, we followed the taxi driver to reception where he handed in our files. A female social worker came to take us to one of the offices in the refugee centre so that they could take our details. There was another lady translating from English to Dutch, while her colleague filled in our forms.

"Are you staying as one family?" the lady asked.

Peter immediately said, "Yes." But I asked what she meant.

"You, Peter and the baby could stay as one family," she said. "Your sister is an adult. She could live with your brother." Lambert was 17 years old.

"No," I said. "My sister and my brother can stay together."

The lady nodded while Peter looked at me as if to say, 'Who do you think you are?' I was on a mission and I didn't trust him at all. I knew I could run to my siblings if things turned out badly with him.

The other thing they told us was that to get by in the Netherlands, we needed to learn how to ride a bike. There are some small towns that don't have public transport, and there you use a bike. Children use bikes when going to school. People ride bikes to work, to the doctor, to shops – everywhere! I learned straight away.

My sister and brother knew how to ride a bicycle already, so for them it was more practice than learning.

After taking all our details, they took us to show where we would live. Everywhere, there were bungalow-style houses. When we reached ours, I shared a room with Peter and baby Lee Ann. My sister shared a room with my brother.

You Must be Joking!

The next day, I couldn't wait to call my parents. At first, my father thought we were joking when I said we were in the Netherlands: "Guys, just tell me you've found a school in Cape Town."

"So, you didn't see that we called from the Netherlands?" I asked. I had not realized that calling from a public phone, the receiver sees it as a private call. I told my father we were not joking. We were in the Netherlands.

"Give me your sister and your brother," he said. "I want to hear them saying the same."

First my brother confirmed it, and then my sister.

"How can I believe you guys?" he asked.

"Okay," I said. "Hold on and let me call you back in a minute."

I saw a guy smoking outside and asked him if he had a mobile phone that I could quickly use to call to Africa. I told him it was an emergency and that I would pay him back his credits. He agreed. I called my father back so that he could see the Dutch phone number. He couldn't believe it. "How did you guys fly there so quickly?" he asked excitedly.

I told him I would send an email and explain every single step and detail of what had happened. When he received it, he was the happiest parent on earth. Later, I learned from my mother that my father spent the night on his knees thanking God for making his dreams come true and asking God to protect his children.

From an Unknown Country

We kept the one-way passports and waited to receive our refugee status ID cards so that we could begin to look for a house outside the refugee centre. Three weeks later, they arrived. When we went to collect them from reception, I looked to see if the details were correct. Under nationality was written 'Onbekend' – a Dutch word meaning 'unknown'. I checked on my brother's and sister's IDs and it was the same. On Peter's, they had put that he was of Burundian nationality. Confused, I asked the immigration officer why they didn't put our nationality too.

"Your case is a bit complicated," the officer said. "You are originally from Burundi but born in Rwanda. That's why we have put unknown."

I went to sit outside. I looked at my ID card again and realized that in every country I had been to, I was given the same status: 'Refugee'. What hurt me more, was that it was even on my birth certificate. I felt that I had no home, that I didn't belong to either Rwanda or Burundi. I was so sad.

After receiving our ID cards, we had to register with various rental housing agencies. When I asked Peter if I could go with him, he shouted at me: "I am now the man of the house. You will follow my rules and conditions."

I looked at him and told him that I was a grown-up woman and that he couldn't give me rules. As I stormed into the kitchen to wash my hands and breastfeed my baby, Peter slapped me so hard in the face, I thought for a moment I could see stars. I tried to defend myself, but he was too strong. I ran into the bedroom, taking my baby to feed her. From that moment, I grew my fingernails so that at least I had some defence.

I cried and cried.

Later, I went into my siblings' bedroom.

"Listen guys, Peter slapped me in the face and I think I need to do something about it."

My sister and brother looked sorry for me, but they didn't know how they could help. I tried to assure them I was going to be okay and would get over it. I asked them just to be there for me as they had promised.

Getting to Know Yvette

I was now ready to deal with the domestic violence, but I didn't know who to tell. I never thought about social workers. I had heard about social workers through Auntie Claudine back in Cape Town, but I had never contacted them.

One afternoon, I was sitting with my sister in the living room of our bungalow and a lady came to say hello. She was tall and light-skinned, and she smiled as if she had met us before. We didn't know who she was, but she seemed happy to see us.

"I heard you guys speak Rwandese?" she said.

"Yeah," I said. "We were born in Rwanda, grew up there, but we are originally from Burundi."

"My name is Yvette and I used to live in this refugee centre, but I moved to my own house just few months ago."

My sister and I introduced ourselves, then made Yvette some tea. It turned out that she was looking for someone who could help remove her braids because they looked old. She asked us if we could do that. We said yes, and a little later we removed the old braids, using a shampoo treatment. That day, Yvette became our best friend, and she still is today.

The next Sunday, Yvette took us to her church. It was a Reformed Church. She introduced us to the pastor who was called John.

"So, are you new in Culemborg?" he asked.

"Yes," I said. "We've been here almost three months."

"Are you also from Rwanda, like Yvette?"

"It's a long story! We were born in Rwanda, grew up there but originally come from Burundi."

"It's all the same, Burundi and Rwanda," Yvette said.

From that day, we became members of Yvette's church and we went there every Sunday.

Domestic Abuse

We had been living in the refugee centre for three months when the housing agency phoned Peter and told him that they had found a house for us. Peter made an appointment behind my back and went to visit the house without me. Two days later, he told me were going together to sign for the house contract.

"A contract?"

"Yes, a house contract," Peter said.

"Did you go and visit the house without telling me?" I asked.

"I told you," he said. "I am the head of the family."

I kept quiet. I didn't want to be beaten.

The day after, I went with him and signed the papers. I looked at the address and registered it in my head, so that I could at least go and check the area and look at the outside of the house. I never kept any of this from my siblings. I told them everything.

Two days later, we took a walk and headed down into the centre of Culemborg. We didn't know where the house was, but we saw a man walking his dog and asked him if he knew the address. We were very close. He pointed four streets ahead to the one we needed. My sister was pushing my little baby Lee Ann in her buggy.

As we approached the street, I saw Peter walking away from the house.

"Where are you going?" he asked.

"To look at the house," I said.

Peter looked embarrassed as he handed me the key to the front door. I took it without saying thank you. When I walked over the threshold, the smell of paint was very strong. Peter had been decorating.

I felt like a stranger. Peter was already painting the house without asking my opinion about the colours, especially for the room for my baby. I wanted to give her a nice room in her first home. I felt useless.

"I am scared that I will get killed in this house" I told my sister.

I cried. My sister wiped my tears. My brother stood in the corner of the room, worried for me.

I liked the house. It had three bedrooms, a spacious spare room for guests, a large kitchen, a living room, dining room, store room, bathroom and toilet.

Later, we went back to the refugee centre. I decided not to say a word to Peter and instead handed him back the house key. He didn't even ask me if I liked the house.

I knew that the council had given us money to buy furniture, so the next day, I asked Peter if we could go together and choose nice things for the house. Peter removed the belt from his trousers and beat me. I screamed, and my siblings came running. Peter opened the door and told them to get into our bedroom and watch him beating me.

Peter took the belt and beat me again. My brother tried to fight him off, but Peter told him he would hit him too. I asked Annie and Lambert to leave and told them I was going to take care of the situation. My baby was 5 months old at the time, so I told my sister to go with baby Lee Ann into her bedroom. I didn't want her to hear all this.

To this very day, I still have the scars from that belt.

Stabbing at the Shadows

I knew that my sister had a soft and fragile heart, but I didn't know that my situation would affect her as drastically as it did. One day, she woke up with a weird look on her face. I didn't know what was going on. Later, she started talking to herself, and running around the house. "Sis, what's wrong?" I asked.

She didn't say a word, but she kept giving me that weird look. Later she went into the kitchen and took a knife.

"Look at that lion!" she shouted. "Look at that snake! I want to kill them all!" She was facing the wall, trying to stab the shadows.

I fought with her to get the knife out of her hands. As my brother came back from chilling outside with his friends, he found us fighting, and asked me what was going on. I told him.

"I know what it is," he said. "Sis is having a tough time seeing you being hurt. She never recovered from all the wars in Burundi, Rwanda and Congo, and those snakes and lions she talks about are the ones we saw in Swaziland. She can't deal with everything in her head and you know how fragile her heart is."

"Sis, what do you want?" my brother and I asked.

"I want to see Mama and Papa."

I knew that the only therapy was for her to see them again. But how? We were still new in the Netherlands. We had no job to get the ticket for her to go to Tanzania. I didn't know what to do, but I kept praying that God would help my sister.

When we moved to the new house, I told Peter that I wasn't leaving my sister in the refugee centre with those problems. Peter said he didn't want any of my siblings at his house. I ignored him and brought my sister to stay with me so that I could take care of her. She was my responsibility. I took her to the hospital, but the treatment they gave her wasn't helping at all. I knew that the only therapy she needed was seeing our parents.

My Sister's Therapy

One day after church, my sister started acting strangely. Pastor John saw that I was worried. He asked me what was wrong, and I told him the whole story, including being a victim of domestic violence. I told him that the only help my sister needed was to go and visit my parents. Little did I know that God's help was on the way!

One day, Pastor John called and said that he wanted to help. I was speechless. All I could do was ask God to bless him and his family.

At this time, my brother and sister had moved out of the refugee camp into an apartment. I felt so happy when I went with them to buy the paint and furniture. They even asked me to choose the paint for the guest room.

"Sis, choose the colour for your room," my brother said, laughing and teasing me.

He knew their place was going to be my refuge.

We painted the house, decorated it, and put furniture in each room. It was a nice apartment with three bedrooms – one for my sister, the other one for my brother, and a spare bedroom, a living room, dining room, kitchen, store room, bathroom, and toilet.

By the end of November 2001, we had all moved into our houses.

During the month of December, my sister prepared for her journey, which was planned for January 2002. We had a lovely first Christmas in Europe – so unlike the one we had the year before in Cape Town. It was cold! We went to church and then later to dinner at Yvette's house.

The week after, at New Year's, we went to Rotterdam where an African party had been organized. I didn't really enjoy it. I was still hurting from Peter's abuses, and the situation with my sister was driving me crazy.

By the first week of January, my sister's travel document was ready. She was due to fly the following week. I asked her to come to my place, so I could help do her hair and prepare her suitcase.

Four days before her trip, she stopped by my house. I was doing my sister's hair in the guest room when I smelled smoke. I hurried downstairs to find that the suitcase with my sister's freshly ironed clothes was empty. I looked in the fireplace. There were the remains of burning clothes. Peter had set fire to them.

I didn't know how to react. This was beyond anything I could have ever imagined. Was I living with the devil? I knew that Peter wasn't that stupid, but he was dangerous. He just wanted to do everything he could to hurt me.

I went back upstairs, not knowing what I was going to tell my sister.

"What was that smell?" she asked.

After a long pause, I told her.

"What can we do?" she asked calmly.

"We should go to your house," I said. I wanted to protect my sister before her trip to Tanzania. "The most important thing is to get you to Tanzania, with or without a suitcase full of clothes." Then I reminded her how lucky she was to be returning to Africa after only six months in Europe. Some people had to wait years before they could do that.

I didn't have any money to help my sister buy other clothes. I didn't even know how much money we had because Peter had all the bank cards and he never let me have access to our accounts, even though we had family income. He had even told me not to open any letter addressed to him. I remember one day trying to open a letter to see his reaction. He slapped me in the face.

At least my sister had a few items of clothing left that she had not planned to take with her.

So, in the second week of January, my sister travelled to Tanzania to visit my parents and to get her therapy.

I knew I had made a good decision.

I was right.

A Bucket of Ice-Cold Water

Just one week after my sister had left for Tanzania, I was sitting in the living room watching MTV, trying to forget my worries. I was already missing my sister.

Peter came in with his manipulative smile. I didn't react.

"You know, I am sorry for everything," he said. "I am sorry for the pain I have caused you. I am sorry for burning your sister's clothes. I am sorry, I am sorry, I am sorry."

I looked at him and didn't say a word. I knew he was up to something, that he wanted something from me. I was right. Peter had filled in a form for child benefit. It had been declined because the mother was the one who had to apply. He knew that if I had filled in that form, I would have access to money of my own because the money had to go into my account (I didn't have one at the time). I didn't know about child benefit because I had grown up without it in Africa, and I didn't have any information about how things worked in Europe. So, I was the one who had to fill in the claim and I was the one who had to open an account in my name for the money.

Peter came and sat beside me, telling me that I would have to give him my bank card when I received the money.

"Why?" I asked.

"You see, we have to pay a lot of bills and I need to use that extra money to top up our income," he replied.

I laughed as if to say, *Hell no!*

I was having a hard time buying clothes, toys and treats for my baby. That was her money, not her father's.

The next day I went to open an account. Peter asked me if he could go with me and I refused. I was given the bank details and these I added to the child benefit forms which I sent off to be processed.

When I opened the account, I asked the bank if I could give them my sibling's postal address so that the card could be sent there, along with all bank statements. I explained why, and the bank agreed.

Peter thought I was so stupid that I would never think of changing the address. I presented myself as meek to avoid fighting with him. He had no idea of my plans. He met me after I had survived so many adventures that he took me for a stupid woman to be beaten, insulted, shouted at, and silenced. How wrong he was! I was about to show him that I was the very opposite of stupid!

Peter knew that the bank card would arrive after five working days. He didn't go anywhere; he stayed at home waiting for the post to arrive. One week after my visit to the bank, he asked if I had received the bank card yet. I told him that I had it, but I had asked my brother to keep it for me. He searched my purse and my handbag. He threw everything up and down, but he couldn't find the bank card.

Late in the evening when I went to the bedroom, I tried to open the door, but Peter had locked it from the inside. He didn't want to let me in, so I went to sleep in the guest room. Later, in the middle of the night, I heard a noise in the bathroom, like water coming from a tap, but I didn't go and see what it was. A few minutes later, Peter opened my door and threw a ten-litre bucket of iced cold water all over me.

I dashed out of the wet bed, my clothes soaking. I cried. I could not believe the abuse I was receiving from this man.

I changed my clothes and went to sleep downstairs in the living room. I locked the door behind me and lay on the couch with my daughter. Did I sleep that night? No, it wasn't the time for that. It was time for me to figure out how I was going to get out of this abuse. It was time, once again, for me to remember how tough and resilient I was – to remember who I really was. It was time to ask for help. I decided that the next day I would call my best friend Yvette and tell her about my situation.

A Comforting Letter

The next morning, the first thing I did was phone Yvette. "Can you please come over here. I need to talk to you."

"Oh my God! I am busy right now. Can I come later?" Yvette said.

"Please! It's urgent."

"Okay, if you insist."

An hour later, Yvette arrived.

"What's wrong? You look sad."

Before I could answer, I burst into tears. "There is something I didn't tell you," I said between sobs.

"What? Are you pregnant?"

"Hell no!"

I went on to tell Yvette about my abusive life with Peter, how I was suffering continual, domestic violence. I told her everything – how Peter would force me into having sex with him, how he would call me names, how he would say that I was only a woman to use for sex but not a woman worth marrying.

"Have you reported this?" Yvette asked.

"No. I don't know where to go."

"You should report him to social services."

That same night, I decided to confide in my other best friend Liliane in Canada. She was so angry that it had taken me so long to tell her. As Yvette had done, she advised me to seek help from the social services.

Two-and-a-half weeks later, Pastor John and I went to pick my sister up from the airport in Amsterdam. I cried when I saw her. It felt like years since I had seen her.

When we reached my sister's place, she opened her suitcase and handed me a gift from my parents and a letter from my father to Pastor John, as well as a letter from my father to me. That letter revealed how sad and heartbroken he was to hear that I was living an abusive life. My father advised me to come out of that relationship.

That letter brought me so much relief. I had been held back by the African mindset that if a woman leaves her man, it is a thing of shame. I hadn't been thinking about my happiness, only what people might say about me. Another thing, I was officially married to Peter and that was my status in the Netherlands. That also had put the brakes on my decision. Nonetheless, I now knew that I didn't love Peter at all and my daughter didn't receive any affection from her father. He never cared about her, so I had no reason for staying.

"I Will Kill You, One Day!"

Weeks passed by and God blessed me when the Dutch authorities started paying me child benefit. It was March and my baby was almost 1 year old.

I told Peter that I wanted to organize a first birthday party for our daughter and he told me that I shouldn't rely on him to help. Thank God the money for the child benefit was there by then. I decided to do it alone and prepare a small party. The 19 March was a weekday, so I decided to hold the party on a Saturday, the 23rd. I invited only a few people; parents with young children and other close friends.

Two days before my baby's birthday party, my sister, Yvette and I made a list and went shopping. On the Saturday, I celebrated my daughter's first birthday. Peter was there, pretending that he had been involved in all the preparation. But that didn't distract me from the joy of seeing my baby blowing out her first candle. And as I always put a smile on my face, even when life gets hard, none of the guests suspected that there was tension between me and the man who was abusing me.

After everybody left, I started cleaning up and putting everything back in order. Peter had escorted some of the visitors out of the house. When he returned, he started yelling.

"You are a prostitute, you bitch! You think you are the man in this house? You think you have won, huh? I am telling you, I will kill you one day!"

He started demonstrating how he would kill me using a gun, how he would wear gloves to protect his identity, how he would throw me in the river. He yelled and yelled, and all the while I just listened. I could see the veins throbbing in his neck.

And then, he approached me. I was standing in the kitchen washing dishes, carrying Lee Ann on my back. I was trying to put her to sleep because she was tired. She had played with other children all day.

Peter pushed me.

"Leave me alone!" I said.

He slapped me, but I pushed him away. That was the first time I had done that. I tried to defend myself by pulling his shirt, but he used his Timberland boots and kicked my leg just under my knees. It hurt me for years afterwards.

I couldn't wait for the next day to go and report Peter to the social services. The social worker recorded everything. From then on, they had a file of my case. I even reported Peter to the police.

Saved by the Bell

One of the things I hated was the fact that I was in the same class as Peter learning the Dutch language. There was no other choice, but I was lucky that my sister and Yvette were also in the same class.

One day, in the month of June 2002, I had gone to my sister's house and returned home late, around 7 p.m.

I knew that after reporting my case to the social worker, they would get in touch with Peter.

That night, I found all the doors – front and back – locked from inside. I rang the bell but there was no response. I could see that the lights were on inside.

I kept ringing the bell, but there was still no response.

Then, around 9 p.m., I went to the police station and told them Peter had refused to let me in the house, and that it was getting late for my baby to go to bed.

They escorted me back and knocked on the door. Again, Peter thought I was the one knocking and he didn't open.

The police shouted and told him to respond. I saw Peter looking through the upstairs bedroom window.

"Open the door or we will break it down!" the policewoman shouted.

The door opened.

When the police asked Peter why he had locked the door, he lied to them and told them that I was drunk. They dismissed this. I didn't even drink alcohol!

"If you ever do this again, we will arrest you!" they said.

When we went inside, Peter turned on me.

"So, you brought the police for me now, huh?"

"Why are you so scared?" I said. "You were the one who said you had nothing to fear from the police!"

"You bitch! I am going to kill you!"

"Don't call me a bitch," I said.

"You are just a hole to have sex with!" he yelled. "You are not a woman to make a wife."

Those words hit me. Every time I had had sex with Peter, that was how he had seen me – as just a hole.

The next day, Peter didn't stay at home during the day. He came back late in the evening. When he returned, he looked weird. I was scared. My baby was playing with her toys in the living room and I was sitting on the couch watching the Oprah Winfrey show. He was about to do something terrible, when I was saved by the bell – by the ringtone on Peter's phone, to be precise.

Peter had run upstairs and then come back with a lighter and a bottle of petrol.

"I'm going to burn your face!"

I thought this was the end. I was about to die.

Just as he was about to act, his phone rang, and he went to pick it up in the corridor, where his jacket was hanging.

I hurried to Lee Ann where she was playing with her toys and picked her up, along with my handbag, which was on the dining table. While Peter was still on the phone, I rushed through the back door, jumped onto my bike, put my baby in her bike seat, and peddled as fast as I could to my siblings' place.

When I arrived, I was in utter panic. I couldn't feel any part of my body. My legs were shaking. My heart was beating as if I had just run a marathon.

"What's going on?" they cried. But it was like talking to a deaf person.

Later, after I had calmed down, I told them how Peter was going to burn my face.

"I'm not going back to him," I said. "It's over and I have had enough."

That was the day I left Peter.

I never returned to my house until I filed for a divorce.

Changing the Locks

The next day, I reported the incident to the social services, to the police, to Yvette, to Pastor John, and my best friend Liliane in Canada. Pastor John told me that they had reported Peter to the police that very day; they suspected that he had a pistol, and Peter was telling people he was looking for me. They had seen him with something that looked like a pistol on his vest.

The police went to search the house. When they searched Peter, they found his phone on his vest. Peter always used to laugh at people who carried their phones in holsters. "They're just village people," he would say. Turns out, he was one of them too!

As I had left my house without any of my clothes, or my baby's, Yvette arrived at my sister's place holding two plastic bags.

"Here are some of my son's clothes," she said. "They're for Lee Ann until we buy her new clothes. Don't look at the colour and say they are for boys!" She also gave me some clothes for myself. "And these are for you. I couldn't find your size in any of mine, but you can use these African clothes. They are big enough."

From that time, Yvette became my daughter's godmother.

The social services arranged an appointment for me to see a lawyer. I was honest with her and told her the truth about not being officially married to Peter, that when I had filled in the resettlement forms, Peter had manipulated me and forced me to say that we were married.

I stayed at my siblings' place for five months before the announcement of the divorce came in November

2002. Peter tried to win me back, even begging me, but I refused. When my divorce was finalized, the courts decided that I should go back home. Peter would have to leave my house and find somewhere else to live.

Before I moved back, I changed all the locks and redecorated everything. The church helped me to find new furniture because I didn't want anything in the house that reminded me of my miserable life with Peter.

At the beginning of December 2002, I went home. As the subsequent days went by, my focus was trying to recover from all my wounds. There was a lot to heal – the traumas of war, exile, abuse, and domestic violence. I really needed time, and I needed people by my side to help me. I didn't want special therapists. All I needed was to be with the people I loved and who loved me. My siblings, my daughter, Yvette, and my other dear friends were there for me and this gave me the platform to start my life all over again. I love them more than anything. If it wasn't for them, I could have ended up depressed or dead.

Love is Born Again

As I recovered, I kept thinking that one day Peter might try to kill me, but God protected me. The child protection services arranged the days when Peter could visit his child, but I can count the days when he did. Now I had to learn a new way of life where I was the one paying the bills. I was receiving income support and since I was trying to recover from all the traumas I had suffered, I asked the council to pay all my bills directly and give me the rest of the money. I didn't want to get into trouble. Everything in Europe is about paying bills, bills, bills. It was all new for me.

Peter had left so many debts that I had to participate in paying half. This is a common problem for women when they separate from their partners. It was time, therefore, to rebuild my life. I was committed to learning Dutch so that I could get back into education. I wanted to go back to college and enjoy the career that I had always wanted since I was young – being a journalist.

One day, in the summer of 2003, I went to Amsterdam to an African-Caribbean party. It had been so long since I had gone out for a dance. I remember my sister stayed with my daughter. It felt like the old days when I used to enjoy myself. It was a year after I had separated with Peter. My confidence was coming back.

While I was on the dancefloor, I met an old friend named Aime. The last time I had seen him was in Zambia. We hugged and hugged. It was a wonderful surprise.

We left the dancefloor and found somewhere less noisy. While we chatted, I saw a guy who looked like a friend we all knew back in Zambia. "That guy looks like Dax," I said to Aime.

"You mean Daxton?" Aime asked.

"Yeah!"

"Didn't you know Dax also lives here in the Netherlands?" Aime asked.

"Don't tell me!" I cried.

As we spoke, I asked Aime to give me Dax's phone number. Later we went back on the dancefloor. It was a wonderful night. I had enjoyed myself a lot!

I spent the next day in bed because I had danced until I dropped.

Later in the evening, I found Dax's number and called him.

"Hallo. Is this Dax?"

"Yes, speaking. Who is this?"

"I don't think you will recognize my voice, because it has been ages," I said. Then I introduced myself.

From that moment, Dax and I talked on the phone day after day, until we started dating.

When I was with Peter, I had thought that love didn't exist anymore.

When I found Dax, I knew that love had been born in me again.

When my Daughter said 'Papa'

That same summer, I was supposed to meet Father Aloyz in Brussels on his way to America. I told Dax that I was going to Brussels and that I was passing where he lived. We planned to meet and say a quick hi. The plan was for me to have a chat with Dax when my train stopped for a while – a quick hallo and a quick kiss on the cheek. This was two weeks after we had started talking on the phone.

On 23 July 2003, Dax and I met at the train station at Rotterdam, the City where he lived. We hugged and hugged. When we started chatting, I decided to catch the next train in an hour's time.

We went to sit in a restaurant near the train station and shared memories. He told me that I hadn't changed. I'd just gained some weight. I told him he hadn't changed either. I asked him about his siblings. We talked about our friends and wondered where they had ended up after fleeing from war zones. It was a wonderful time.

Several minutes before I boarded the train to Brussels, we set a date for Dax to come and visit me at my house.

We kissed goodbye on the cheek.

I boarded the train.

We both waved to each other.

Then I left for Brussels.

In Brussels, I had a quick meeting with Father Aloyz. I thanked him for everything he had done for us. Since we had left Zambia in 1999, we had only kept in touch by email. I wanted to meet him in person and thank him for having opened the doors for me and my siblings. He was the one who had given me the chance to continue my studies.

I told Father Aloyz all about the abuse I had endured from the father of my daughter. The tears were running from his eyes as I told my story.

It was great to see him, and he even gave me some money, which I used to buy new furniture and decorate the rooms I had not altered since the separation between me and Peter. I completely removed every trace of Peter's presence from my house.

After a while, Dax and I fell in love. There was love everywhere. Love in the house, love outside the house, love on the street, love in the supermarket – love, love, love, everywhere.

Three months after we had started dating, we decided to tell our family members. I told my siblings and my two best friends, Yvette and Liliane. Dax told his siblings, then introduced me to his sisters on the phone. They lived in Canada. He introduced me to his friends and I introduced him to mine.

We started going out in public. We had nothing to hide because we were both in love. I had found the man of my dreams – someone who didn't hide the fact that he loved me, someone who could take jokes and laugh, someone that I could tell a joke to and answer me back with another one, someone who loved my daughter as if she was his very own. He was a funny guy. He was handsome and kind; he was a gentleman. He had everything that I ever wanted in a man.

One day, I had no coffee for breakfast and I went to the store. When I came back, I heard my daughter calling Dax, "Papa!"

"Wait a second!" I said. "Did I hear Lee Ann calling Dax 'Papa'?"

Again, Lee Ann called Dax 'Papa'. I was confused. I had never heard that word from my baby's mouth. I remember when I had been with Peter, Lee Ann called her father 'Mama' and Peter used to yell that he wasn't her 'Mama'. He would force her to say the word 'Papa', but Lee Ann would say, 'Mama'!

Dax, seeing me looking confused, approached me in the kitchen while I was preparing breakfast.

"I told Lee Ann to call me Papa," he said.

I was simply speechless. All I could think of doing was giving him a kiss. So, I did!

"Do you mind if Lee Ann calls me Papa?" he asked.

I burst into tears and thanked him for what he had done for my daughter.

"Lee Ann shouldn't be affected by the problems between you and her father," he said. "I decided to give her what she doesn't have."

I will never forget that day.

A New Arrival

Our first Christmas and New Year were crazy. It was 2003 and we planned a New Year's party at my place.

Dax invited his friends. My siblings were there, as well as my two cousins Sonia and Nadia who had come to visit me from France. Everybody was elated. I was the happiest woman on the earth.

That Christmas, Dax asked me to give him a gift – a child. *Oh God!* I thought. I knew I was in love, but I was scared of being hurt again. Dax showed me the meaning of love; he cherished me and respected me, but still I was frightened.

In the end, I told him. He replied that he understood the pain and the trauma of my previous relationship, but he promised to take care of me and the baby. He begged, begged, and begged. I told him I would think about it.

I decided to say yes, even though I knew that I was taking a risk.

One day at Easter time, I shared the good news with Dax that I was pregnant. From that day, I came to see how a pregnant woman can be treated like a queen. My hormones had changed, and I didn't want to see Dax that much. He was living one hour from where I lived, but at the weekend he would come and spend time with me.

He was very understanding. He knew that my hormones had changed. Sometimes, I would think of telling him not to come the next weekend, but all he ever wanted was to be there for me, even when I was mad at him, even when my face turned ugly. I felt so sorry for Dax. He was scared that I wouldn't be myself again after giving birth.

I had asked the gender of the baby. I was having a boy. We started thinking of names. Dax loved Lenny Kravitz, so I asked him if we could name our son

Lenny – the same first letter as his sister Lee Ann. Dax liked it. So, Lenny it was! The baby was due to be born 30 November 2004.

By September, I had finished buying everything we needed. With my hormones now raging, I hated my house, so I stayed most of the time with my siblings, until one week before the baby came. The plan was for me to go to my house, arrange the baby's room, wash the baby's clothes, arrange them in the wardrobe, then return to my siblings' house.

During the morning of 17 November, I started having some contractions. My brother was walking through the corridor on his way to college. Without hesitating, he called in sick at the college, then called my sister who was already on the train on her way to college. Then he called Dax who was at work. My sister came straight home. On her way, she called Yvette.

I called a taxi which took me to my house, where my sister joined me.

Two hours later, my waters broke. My sister panicked. She knocked on my neighbour's door. She was a taxi driver. Within ten minutes, the taxi driver rushed me to the hospital at Tiel.

Everything went so quickly. The nurses checked me and said that the baby was ready to come out. They took me to the delivery room. Within fifteen minutes, my baby boy was born at 1 p.m.

Dax was still on his way to the hospital. He was supposed to start his holidays in a week, but our baby had arrived two weeks early. All my children arrived two weeks ahead of schedule!

I saw Dax and my siblings enter the room where I was sleeping. In his one hand, Dax held some lovely flowers; in the other, Lee Ann. He was the happiest man ever. My siblings were happy for me too. Lee Ann was then 3 years and 8 months old. She was sucking her thumb and looking at her brother where he was sleeping in a baby bed.

The day after, I went back home to find the house clean and organized – Yvette and my sister had prepared everything and had done a great job.

Enrolling at College

A month later, the day after Christmas, it was my sister's birthday and her engagement party. My sister had a boyfriend who was living in the UK. He had proposed to her in the summer of 2003 and we had planned their engagement party for one year later in December on my sister's birthday.

It was a lovely day and I felt so blessed to see my little sister making the first step towards married life. I was enjoying being a mother, especially with the full support of Dax. I was the happiest woman on earth. Surely it couldn't last.

Dax's visa had now run out and he wasn't allowed to continue living in the Netherlands. We decided that Dax should move to another country – somewhere in Europe, where we could visit each other easily. It was hard for us to make that decision, but it was better for Dax and I didn't want to be selfish.

When our son was 4 months old, Dax left. We kept in touch. He called me every day and I called him often. When my son was 8 months old, I went to visit him, and everything seemed okay. He was just waiting to get his visa.

I became very busy. I was looking after two kids and was still going to learn Dutch because I wanted to achieve the high level which would allow me to do my journalism course. Meanwhile, Dax's friends visited me often. I visited them too. We all hoped that Dax would come back to live in the Netherlands once his visa was sorted. My sister was then preparing for her wedding which was to take place in the summer of 2006.

One day, I had to register for college at an open evening event. When I arrived there, I looked at all the courses but there was none for journalism. I approached a lady who was advising people about the courses available at that college. She told me that I wouldn't be accepted to do the course unless I attained another level of Dutch knowledge. I asked her about the administration course and she discouraged me from doing it, saying I wouldn't find a job with an administration qualification. She showed me two other courses, Home Care and Catering. She told me I would get a job if I did one of those two courses. I insisted that I wanted to do the administration course, and after that, journalism. I simply wanted to fulfil my heart's desires and become a journalist. I told her I enjoyed caring for people and I liked to cook, but I didn't want to do that for a career.

I couldn't believe what the woman was saying to me. I remembered how my father used to tell us that, when you are a foreigner in a country, there will be many opportunities, but priority will always be given to the citizens of that country. I was living what my father used to tell me as young girl.

I decided to go for a one-year course as a catering assistant because I really didn't like the thought of home care. I had a plan to finish it and then do my dream course.

I registered to start the following September.

My Sister's Wedding

Finally, Dax's visa got sorted and he came to my sister's wedding in August 2006. I was so happy. I was achieving something by preparing my sister's wedding, something which made my parents proud. I was happy to be with Dax. And I had my two precious children running all over the place, both looking healthy and happy. I couldn't believe how lucky I was.

The day before my sister's wedding, I had a lot of friends and family visiting from all over the world – France, Belgium, Canada, USA, Italy, UK and Germany. Only my parents were missing; they were refused a visa for their daughter's wedding.

That night was crazy. Everyone was preparing for the big day. My sister had moved in with me and all her five bridesmaids were to spend the night at my place doing their hair and make-up with the help of a hired stylist. The groom and his groomsmen were all at Yvette's place and that's where they spent the night.

The day of the wedding was 26 August 2006, a Saturday. I will never forget the moment I saw my sister walking down the stairs from the bedroom, wearing a long white dress, her face covered with a very long veil, her bridesmaids beside her. They all entered the limo waiting for them outside my front door. I went outside and saw everyone on the street watching my sister, including my neighbours. I burst into tears of joy. Later, I shed more tears when I saw my brother holding my sister's hand, walking her down the aisle. I remembered in Tanzania how my father had given me the responsibility of taking care of them. I felt very blessed and proud of myself.

We had a fine church service, reception, and party, with lovely people around us. We spent all night dancing and the next day everyone came to my place for an after-party that lasted almost three days. The last guest went home on Tuesday. Dax left on Thursday, two days after everyone else.

Heartbroken Again

September came knocking at our door and it was time for me to go back to reading books. My daughter was due to go to school as well. I had found day-care for my son, and in September I started college.

I became a busy mum who went to college every day and took care of the kids and the house. I had a very busy schedule. I would put my kids on the bike, take them to school and to day-care, ride my bike to the train station, and go to college. At the end of the day, I would pick up my kids from school and day-care, get home, make dinner, prepare my children for bed, and then get down to my studies. Sometimes it was hard for me in the winter when I had both kids on the bike, one at the front and the other at the back. It was clearly time to work on getting my driving licence.

As the days went by, Dax's silence became deafening. I called and called. I sent text messages and emails, but there was no answer. When I rang, his phone started going straight to voicemail. Weird. I began to wonder if Dax was even alive.

I called Dax's brother and asked him if he had spoken to Dax. He told me that they had recently spoken. At least I now knew he was alive. But why was he not answering my messages? Something was wrong.

I started doing my own investigation and discovered that Dax was having an affair with another woman. They were even about to have a child together. I was 100 per cent sure about the information, because it came from someone who knew all his movements. I was devastated and disappointed and I cried every day, although it didn't stop me going to college.

A week after I had heard the news about Dax, I woke up, switched on my computer and sent him a short email message:

> Hope you are doing okay. Myself and the kids, we are doing great and I thank God for that. I just wanted to let you know that I have heard about you having an affair with someone else, and I want to wish you good luck. The only thing I want to ask is that you remember we have a son together who will need to know you. Take care.

The same afternoon, I took some breadcrumbs, put them in a small sandwich bag and went to sit on a bench beside the water. I threw the small pieces of bread into the water and fed the ducks. I reminded myself that I was lucky to be in the Netherlands. I had spent days and nights in the bush trying to escape certain death. I had escaped Peter's violence, and an abusive life in Zambia when I had refused to get married at a young age. I remembered the Tsunami in Mozambique and the lions and tigers in the forests of Swaziland. Right now, it was a tough time for sure, but I counted myself the luckiest woman on earth.

I looked at myself and saw what a strong woman I had become. I saw a fighter, an intelligent woman, a caring and good mother, an organizer, a planner, and an adviser. I saw everything that I associated with being a real woman.

I looked far away into the distance. I had my future in front of me. I had two precious kids to take care of and bring up. I had to take care of myself because I knew that someone still needed me.

Yes, I was heartbroken, but I had lost the love of just one man, not the love of everyone who cared for me. I still had my kids, my parents and my siblings who loved me unconditionally. I still had my friends who loved me. The past wasn't equal to the future. I was looking ahead.

I committed myself to working hard and putting 120 per cent into bringing up my kids, doing well at college and taking care of myself. I was a single mum and I knew that wasn't going to be easy. It was a full-time and even an extra job, but I was ready to face the challenge.

Dax had showed me that I still had love in me and that I could be loved, and I respected and thanked him for that. I had the opportunity of going to college and I recognized that sometimes an opportunity will knock only once, so it was up to me use it or lose it. I didn't want to live with regrets. I had found myself at last.

The Worst News

Christmas 2006, I was alone in my house with my kids. I was still broken-hearted, but I was ready to start my new plans.

I celebrated New Year in Belgium with my brother and some friends. My sister had gone to be with her husband in the UK. Before the year ended, I said a prayer and asked God to give me strength, and to protect me in the new and challenging life I was ready to start. I had no idea that within two months' time I would lose someone special – the person who helped me to become who I was and who I am today.

One Sunday morning, in February 2007, my mother flashed me on my mobile and I quickly called her back. She picked up, but she didn't sound well. "Pray for your father. He has been taken to the hospital and it's not looking good."

"What's wrong with him?" I asked.

"I don't know. He is vomiting blood."

I had spoken to my father the day before and he had told me he was preparing to go to my uncle's wedding. My uncle Bernard had flown from the USA to get married in Burundi and my father had a big part in the wedding.

Before I could ask for more information from my mother, I ran out of credit.

I didn't think about the bill. I quickly picked up my house phone and called my mother back.

"Call me back later. I am helping your father here," my mother said.

I called my brother straight away. He had gone for a weekend to Belgium and I asked him to pray for our father, adding that he was very sick.

My sister was at my place, braiding the hair of a friend who had come to visit me.

Later, the phone rang. I picked up thinking it was my mother. It was my friend Aime, just calling to say hi. I was upstairs in my bedroom and I told him my father was in the hospital that he wasn't doing well. Then, downstairs I suddenly heard my sister screaming and crying. My Auntie had just called on my sister's phone and shared that my father had passed away. I started screaming too. I told Aime that my father had just died.

I went downstairs and held my sister.

We all cried.

We cried, cried, cried, and cried.

After ten minutes, I took a deep breath and called a friend who was with my brother in Belgium. I passed on the bad news and I asked him not to tell him but to get him back to the Netherlands. I wanted my brother to find out when he was home.

A minute later, I called my best friend Yvette and told her too and asked her if she could inform those who knew us. Within fifteen minutes, Yvette was at my house comforting me and my sister. Soon my house was full of people, most of them from church. Pastor John was one of them.

My sister and I tried to be strong, but it wasn't easy for us to understand that my father had gone forever. We needed our brother, but he had called to say it would be thirty minutes before he would be home. Yvette had taken the call and asked my brother to come straight to my house.

Yvette told me and my sister to go and take a shower. While we were getting dressed, I heard the bell ringing. It was my brother and he was with a group of fifteen of our friends who had travelled with him from Belgium. They had wanted to come and surprise me.

My brother opened the living room and found a crowd of people. He was confused and rushed upstairs to my bedroom. We hugged him and burst into tears.

"Dad is gone."

My brother held us and we kept hold of each other. My sister and I were crying but my brother stayed strong and comforted us. We were all in shock. We were devastated. It was as if a great hole had opened in our hearts – a hole that nothing could fill.

My father had been a friend to all his children. He was my inspiration. He was intelligent. He was the funniest Dad ever. He was a good husband to my mother. He had a big heart. He was everything you could imagine a kind person to be. He had returned to his country after an exile lasting thirty-five years (apart from 1993 when we all went there, but then had to leave after two months because of the war). It had been time for my father to enjoy his country and feel at home. But now he was gone.

My siblings and I were all students and we had no job. Where were we going to find the money to buy the tickets to fly to Burundi for the funeral? We didn't know what to do.

Later, Yvette called us. We followed her outside where she was talking with Pastor John and another family friend from church named Theo. Pastor John and Theo told us that they were going to fund our flights to Bujumbura for our dad's funeral and that my kids were going to stay with Yvette. I felt like I was dreaming. There was nothing to say to these wonderful people apart from thanking them and asking God to bless them.

My Father's Funeral

The next day, we went to the Rwandan embassy for our visas. We had to pass through Rwanda because we had travel documents which didn't allow us to travel straight to Burundi.

The visa was granted as a matter of priority, and Pastor John booked our tickets for the next day, Tuesday. On 6 February 2007, we flew to Kenya and from Kenya we connected to our flight to Rwanda. We reached Rwanda on the morning of the 7th, arriving at Kigali Airport. Albert, Yvette's brother, was waiting for us. We hugged Albert as if we had known him for years, but it was the first time we had met him. We hurried downtown to eat something before continuing to Bujumbura.

Late in the afternoon, we headed to Burundi in a Toyota RAV4 that Albert had arranged for us. We had to pay $150 to the driver. We didn't manage to get to Bujumbura on the same day because it wasn't safe on the road, so we checked into a hotel after we had crossed the border from Rwanda to Burundi at Kayanza. We left the next morning.

Around 11 a.m. on 8 February, we reached my parent's home where we were going to spend several days. A lot of people were sitting silently outside. Everyone was in shock. It was then that it hit me: my dad really had gone. I still couldn't believe it until we entered the house and saw my mother sitting there, looking weak and hopeless. My siblings and I had promised each other that we wouldn't cry when we hugged our mum. We went to comfort her. She started crying as we held her.

That same afternoon, my uncle Sophonie – who was still living in Tanzania – arrived with two of his children, Richard and Mediatrice. When we saw him, we burst into tears. He was Dad's only brother and he looked exactly like my father. He told jokes like my father. We simply couldn't hold it together.

In the evening, I called my auntie's husband and asked him what had happened to my father. I didn't remember even one time when my father told me he was sick – and I had talked to him the day before he died.

"When your father came back from Tanzania," my uncle said, "he looked sick, but he said that he wasn't sick. He looked like someone who had liver problems. However, when I asked him if he was sick, he told me that he had no complaints ever, no pain either."

On 10 February, we paid our last respects to my father, a last goodbye. We escorted my father on his final journey with dignity. We were accompanied by a crowd of people, which demonstrated what he really meant to people, with that big heart he had. He had fought in life. He had fought for his family and his country. He had helped numerous people from different tribes, religions, and countries.

I had no doubt he was going to heaven.

In fact, I knew he was already there.

After the funeral we heard people giving testimonies about how they were helped by my father. It filled me with hope that he was somehow still alive in each one of us, and that he was going to watch over us.

I sat in the car heading to the cemetery. Our car was behind the one transporting my father's body. I remembered the last day I was in Burundi, when I had gone to meet my family for the first time – the family that I didn't get the chance to know because of the war. I remembered all the bad times in the war. I looked at my father's coffin and realized that I had no good memories of my country of origin. Every memory was tinged with sorrow. To this day, this still hurts me.

The Best of Men

Three weeks after my father's death, we had already returned to the Netherlands and organized a church ceremony to pray for my father. We invited our friends and family to be with us that day. I stared at my father's picture at the front, surrounded by candles, and I began to reflect.

I had lost a love that wasn't from just any man; it was from my hero. I had lost a love that was unconditional; no matter what the circumstances. I had lost the love of the man who helped me to become the person I am now. He was the man who showed me the value of an education. He was the man who gave me the responsibility for taking care of my two siblings at a young age. He was the man who showed me the value of love, the man who respected me, the man who taught me how to help and save peoples' lives, the man who protected me.

I had lost a dear father.

My father had done a wonderful job on this earth and his name wasn't going to disappear just like that. He had left fighters who had his pure blood – his children. He had done so many different things that at least one of us could continue doing for other people around the world. I wasn't interested in politics like my father, but I had another part of him – a big heart for helping, inspiring, and encouraging others. It was going to be hard for me to move on without my father. I needed God to help me to accept losing him and move on, because there was a bright future for me.

There was something that helped in this – my father was buried in the country where he had been born and his dream of his children living in Europe had come true. That's what he wanted. He was resting in peace now, of that I was sure.

Busier and Busier

In May that year, I received my driving licence. Two months later, I completed my catering assistance course at a high level. I had already registered for the next course in September. That was to be for administration. I didn't give up. I wanted to do what I enjoyed.

During that time, I had a student loan but it wasn't enough to pay the bills, take care of the kids and pay off the debts that Peter had left. This time, it was going to be more challenging as a single mum.

I applied for a part-time job as a night waitress in one of the local restaurants, about twenty minutes away. By then, my sister had left the Netherlands and had joined her husband in Dublin. My brother came to live with me. At least I had someone to stay with my kids, because I had now started the part-time job. I was organized and had set my goals.

I went for it. I would wake up at 6 a.m., prepare my kids, prepare myself, have our breakfast, drive my kids to school and my son to day-care. I would then drive to the train station, park my car, and take the train to college. I would come back at 5 p.m., pick up my kids at the after-school club, get home, prepare dinner, eat dinner, leave my kids in their pyjamas before I left for my part-time job which I had to start at 7:30 p.m. I would leave at 7 p.m. so as not to be late. I finished work around 11 p.m. or midnight. I would drive home in the dark, returning at about half-past midnight. I would take a shower and fall exhausted into my bed. Then the whole routine began again at 6 a.m. I was lucky that my brother worked during the day, leaving him free to look after my kids in the evening.

Thank God I didn't work at the weekends. That was when I would clean and organize my house. I went to the gym on Saturday and Sunday. I made time for my kids who rarely saw me during the week. And because of that busy schedule, I learned to do my make-up while I sat in the train on my way to college. I was a good reader, but I had to drop reading books because I had no time. Now my kids are older, thank God I have rediscovered my reading habits. I liked partying, but now I was responsible for raising my kids. I also liked clubbing, but that wasn't possible either. I didn't want to lose any momentum in my life because I knew that later, in my old age, I would regret it.

Now that I was so busy, I came up with a plan. I had many friends who loved me and who cared about me. I started organizing parties at my house instead of going out. I had enough space to host more than thirty people. I would organize and plan a surprise birthday party for one of my friends. I would create something to celebrate. I would cook for them and ask them to bring some drinks, or I would buy food and drink if I had enough money. Then we would party the whole weekend! We called ourselves I-CREW; 'I' stood for 'Inshuti', a word in Kinyarwanda which means 'friends'. It was a friend's crew. If it was the month of May, we would organize some games, especially basketball. In January, I always organized a party for everyone in which we would pray for the New Year and ask God to protect us.

Having these people around me helped me a lot. They may not have realized how much it helped me, but they contributed so much to keep me strong, to help me realize that I could make it without a lover in my life. They released the organizer and adviser in me and made me aware that I was a caring person and a mother. Through them, I saw that I had people who loved me. I will always be grateful to them.

I Need a Holiday

In August 2008, my brother and I drove to Lyon in France. He had a girlfriend who lived in Lyon and we were going to visit her family. It was a long, ten-hour drive. We agreed that I would drive for four hours, and my brother would drive the rest.

On the highway, I told my brother that I was working so hard that I needed a holiday. I asked him if he could stay with my kids. My brother was okay with that. He even told me that he had wanted to tell me to do the same thing.

I had no place yet in my mind where I could go on holiday. I thought I might go and visit my mother in Burundi, but it had always been hard to think of going there. All my memories were of it being a very unsafe place.

Wait a second, I said to myself. *I think I need a holiday in Cape Town.*

I had found my holiday destination!

When I went back to work and asked my manager if he could add more hours for me to work at the weekends, saying that I wanted to save for my next holiday in a year's time. The manager was cool with that and added five more hours at the weekends to my normal weekly schedule.

I started saving for my holiday, planning for July 2009.

In the middle of January 2009, I found a message from Dax in my inbox, saying that he wanted to talk to me and see the kids. I told him that I was still at the same address and that he only had to let me know when he was coming. I really needed to hear from his own lips what I had done to him that was so wrong.

Three weeks later, Dax came to my house on a Saturday. The kids were happy to see him after two-and-a-half years. Before we talked, he took them outside to play in the snow. When he came back inside, he began to talk.

"I know this sounds crazy, but I would like to apologize for the pain I have caused you. I regret what I have done. I regret not having you in my life as my wife. What happened was not something I planned. I never wanted to hurt you. Please, I need your forgiveness."

I asked him if he thought I had done anything wrong to him.

"What happened had nothing to do with you," he said.

I told him that I had forgiven him a long time ago, that I had moved on and that I wanted us to be friends, the way we used to be before we fell in love.

"Just remember we have a son together," I said.

"Listen," he said. "Remember I was the one who asked Lee Ann to call me her father? We share a daughter and that daughter is Lee Ann. When the time comes, she can know the truth, but I will always consider her a daughter to me." Dax looked at Lee Ann playing with her brother Lenny. "Look at her now," he said. "She is so innocent. Never say that we only have a son together. We have a daughter too."

Those words touched me deep within my heart. I always respected Dax for saying that. From that time on, I felt a great sense of relief and agreed to stay friends with Dax.

My Favourite City

The summer was fast approaching and so was my holiday. In June, I went to the bank and collected the money I had saved. I went to the travel agency and booked my flight to Cape Town. There was one cheap ticket, stopping over in Cairo (Egypt). I bought it because I had always wanted to see the pyramids and the Nile.

On 20 July, just a few days after the schools had closed for holidays, I flew to Cairo. I spent a day there visiting the Egyptian museums and the Nile river. I even paid someone to take me to the pyramids on a horse. I was really living the life.

The next day, I flew to Johannesburg. I stayed there for a week in a bed and breakfast belonging to a family friend. I went to visit Stella's mother and her four siblings in Pretoria. We recalled the time we spent sleeping in the bush when we were hiding at their grandfather's place back in 1993 during the civil war in Burundi. I was so happy to see them alive. Stella is now in Canada with her parents. Her sisters and brothers who were in Pretoria are now in Australia.

After one week in Johannesburg, I travelled to the lovely Cape Town, my favourite city – the city which gave me the most beautiful gift in the world, my daughter. When I landed there, tears poured down my face. It felt like coming home.

I didn't tell Auntie Claudine, Lee Anne, or Patty that I was coming to Cape Town. I wanted to surprise them.

When I went to see Lee Anne and Patty at UCT, they couldn't believe it. The first thing they asked me was if I had brought little Lee Ann with me. I told them that I couldn't afford to bring my children.

Later, I surprised Auntie Claudine. I was sad to see that her life had not changed at all since I had left Cape Town. It hurt me that she was still living a tough life. She had adopted a little boy, in addition to her own five boys. I was so touched by her big heart. I knew that one day I would do something to help her.

Two weeks before I returned to the Netherlands, I decided to go first to Zambia. My best friend Louise was graduating that same August, so I flew to Lusaka. When I arrived, I met Felix, one of my childhood friends. We grew up together as refugees in Rwanda. He was also living a tough life, and that touched me a lot too. I now had two people on my heart to help on my return to the Netherlands.

In Lusaka, I remembered all I had suffered while living at Adam's house. I thanked God for helping me to see that I was a fighter and that I could make it in life, even at that young age. I was happy to see Louise graduating for her degree. I spent only a week in Lusaka, then I flew back to Durban to visit my uncle.

Time to be Decisive Again

Four weeks later, my holiday was over, and I had to return to the Netherlands, back to my busy life. I went back to work and when I received my two month's salary, I split it in two; sending 500 Euros to Auntie Claudine, and the other 500 to Felix. I helped them both to start their small business.

In January 2010, I received my Dutch citizenship. I couldn't wait to apply for my first passport. It was going to be my first passport since I was born. I really wanted people to ask me what my nationality is. I remember how my sister and I would joke about it.

"Ask me." I would tell my sister.

"What is your Nationality?"

"Dutch." I would proudly respond.

I thought then that life might become easier. The economy in most European countries had deteriorated during the recession. I was almost done with my administration course and I was still working as a waitress in the restaurant.

One day in March, after my daughter's ninth birthday, I went to work only to hear some bad news. That night, my manager told me that business was slowing down and that I only had only one month left. I was confused, but I kept my faith. The scholarship I had received was for people under 30 years old. I had turned 30 that same month, on 15 March. In June, my scholarship had to stop because I was also finishing with my administration course.

In April, I lost my job. Even though I was now unemployed, that same month God blessed me and I became an auntie. My brother had a daughter with his girlfriend and they named her Olga. She was my first niece. I always wanted to have someone call me Auntie. God had brought me an angel.

I remember the day I went to see her in Belgium. I prayed to God while I was holding her in my arms, looking into her face. I asked God to let my niece be my angel and bring miracles to her from heaven. At that time, my brother had to move to Belgium to be there for his child.

In June, I completed my course and the money from my scholarship stopped. I seemed to have sunk so deep in the river that I didn't know how to come out of it. I went to register for benefit, but my claim was rejected. They said that I had finished studying and that now I had to find a job.

I failed to pay the bills. I failed to take care of my children. I failed to pay the rent. I failed in everything. I had a little help from some members of the church and my siblings gave me some money, but that wasn't enough. It could only help me buy food for my kids, but not pay the bills.

I tried to be strong for my kids, but it was hard for me to handle it, especially when I started receiving letters saying I had to leave the house because I had failed to pay the rent. Reminders to pay bills came every day, but I had no solution.

One day, I was talking on the phone with my brother. He was very concerned about my situation and he advised me to move to Belgium and try to get a job there. Things came to a head when I was given a deadline to leave the house. I had nowhere to go, but an old lady from the church called Tante Conny decided to give me a place to stay until I sorted things out. I had told her that I had decided to move to Belgium to begin a new life there. There were only a few weeks left before the kids had their summer holidays.

When the term ended, I acted decisively, just as I always had done in the past.

That August, I moved to Belgium and stayed at my brother's place in Aalst.

A new chapter of my life was about to begin.

Me at Cape Town Airport (July 2009)

Me and my kids, Lee Ann and Lenny. (2021)

Chapter 13
FEELING THE PINCH

I waited for Christmas and New Year to pass before looking for a job. At the time, I was staying at my brother's place with his girlfriend and my little niece Olga. They lived at Aalst, about a half an hour drive from Brussels. My brother went to work every day and his girlfriend went to college to study nursing. They were very busy. I took care of baby Olga and enjoyed every moment of it. I loved being an auntie. Finding a job proved difficult; the recession meant that many people were out of work.

One Sunday evening, a very good friend of mine, called Henriette, phoned and asked if I wouldn't mind working as a cleaner in peoples' houses. Even though I was looking for a job in administration, there was no way I was going to refuse work at that time. It was a great opportunity to grab with both hands. I passed the interview, and a week later started work. I had five different families that I worked for, including one British family who loved me very much. All five houses were in Brussels. I was lucky that I still had my small car from the Netherlands to help me get around.

Life was very busy now; I still had to help my brother take care of their baby, so I would first drop my niece off at day-care, then make my way to work, then pick her up after work. My children went to a school just two minutes from where we lived, which was fortunate. They walked themselves there and back.

Two months later, I decided to look for my own place so that all of us could enjoy our personal space. As I started searching, I found a house for rent around the corner from where my brother lived. As it turned out, the landlord was the same as my brother's, so he said yes. Within a week, I had moved into my own home with my children.

Now I was truly getting my life back. I had a job, even if it wasn't what I really wanted as a career, but at least it helped pay the bills and feed my kids.

Looking for Another Job

One day, I started suffering from chest pains. I had no idea what the cause was. When I started my cleaning job, I sneezed every day, but I didn't know why, except that it was every time I used the spray before I started cleaning. At times I thought I was simply catching a cold. I went to see a doctor. I told him I was having some bad chest pains. He asked me if my job involved lifting heavy things, and I said no.

I described the kind of job I was doing. The doctor gave me some tests which revealed that I was allergic to the household cleaning product. I would have to tell my clients that they needed to buy neutral cleaning products. None of my clients wanted to spend money on this, so they decided to look for someone else. I lost all five clients and my job.

I then went to one interview after another, but there was nothing. Every employer blamed it on the poor state of the economy.

One day, I went to an agency called Randstad and told them I was looking for a job. They asked me if I could do care work and I said yes. They said they had only two hours each day for me, working with a vulnerable young guy who had some physical disabilities. I decided to go for it.

I went to meet the person in question. His name was Erik. His parents showed me what I had to do to help him. They trained me to use Erik's equipment and to take their son to his activities. Erik was a smart guy; he worked as a camera man. I signed the contract for ten hours a week and started in July 2011.

I enjoyed working with Erik; he was mature, just like me. We always chatted about important matters. I was so connected to him that I felt I wasn't working just for the money, but because I really enjoyed helping someone who really needed it. I would drive Erik to places where he had to film events. People always wanted to know if I was a support worker or just a friend to Erik. We had agreed that we would speak English with each other rather than Flemish, so that he could improve his English. We would go to restaurants and have nice meals together.

I loved caring for Erik, but I was only working ten hours a week. I lived in Belgium as a Dutch citizen and had no support from the government to top up on my income. So once again, life became tough but this time I said, "Enough is enough!" I went back to the work agency to ask them if they had any more hours. They replied that I was going to lose two hours from the ten that I was already doing. The agency had difficulties paying their workers, so they were reducing the number of hours.

I struggled to pay the bills. I would pay half the rent to the landlord but fail to pay the rest. I had to take care of my kids, buying them food to take to school. My children also needed new clothes because in Belgium, kids don't wear uniforms. I began to fail to provide these things.

I cried every day and night, convinced that God had forgotten me. I didn't know anybody who would listen. There was no one to help me. I was an outsider, all alone in a foreign city.

All You Have to Do is Ask!

One day, I went to meet a lady who had brought some Christmas gifts for my kids, given to her by my best friend Yvette. I had to meet her at Brussels Midi Train Station. I got a lift from my brother and he dropped me at the station before heading off for his nightshift. I met the lady, who handed over the gifts. When I went to buy my ticket home, I noticed that I had wrongly counted my coins. I was 30 cents short.

I had no idea what to do, so I simply stayed in the station hall. I looked at everyone passing by; some going about their business, others chatting and laughing. I saw people meeting and hugging their loved ones, looking so happy.

Where was I going to find the 30 cents? I studied the faces of those nearby to see if there was anyone I recognized. Maybe I could ask someone for the money? I felt as if I was beginning to lose my mind.

I went to sit on a bench inside the station. I took a newspaper and started flipping through the pages, but my eyes were not focused on any of the words. After two hours, I was feeling hopeless. It was a freezing December night and I was feeling very cold. I stood up and walked around the station to warm myself. It was then that two guys came up to me.

"You look beautiful. Where do you come from?" one of them asked.

"Holland."

"No, I mean originally."

"I am from Burundi, but I was born and grew up in Rwanda." I am always specific when it comes to this question because sometimes people start asking me questions about Burundi, which I don't really know.

One of the two guys said that he came from Rwanda and that his name was Bosco. I asked him to speak in Kinyarwanda. He agreed, at which point I knew he wasn't lying. The other guy was from one of the Western African countries. I don't remember which. Out of respect for this guy, Bosco and I spoke French.

As we chatted, I decided to tell them that I had been sitting for two hours in the station hall and I was in short of 30 cents to complete my train ticket.

"30 cents? A beautiful woman like you should not be lost and cold just because of 30 cents. Asking won't cost you anything. No one can harm you for simply asking for help when it's just 30 cents," said Bosco.

Bosco and his friend didn't just give me 30 cents. They gave me 2 Euros. It was a bonus!

I took my train, went back home, and hid the Christmas gifts for my children from Yvette (their godmother). I wanted to wait until Christmas before they opened them.

I stayed in touch with Bosco, but later, when I lost my phone, I also lost his contact details. I don't know where he ended up, because he had no visa to stay in Belgium and the last time I spoke to him he was trying to go to Canada. I hope one day to meet him and thank him for saving my life. I hope he will come across this book and find our story.

Lolo's Suggestion

On New Year's Eve, just one hour before the end of 2011, I went into my bedroom and put on my favourite Gospel songs by Don Moen. I kept singing the one where they sing that God will make a way where there seems to be no way, because he works in ways we can't see. I spent forty-five minutes singing. Then I prayed to God.

"Lord, I know you are a wonderful father to me and I know you love me so much, and that you have good plans for me but I can't see any of these plans, even though I know that you work in ways I can't see. So, Lord, I put my life in your hands and ask you to show me what plans you have for me. I need you to give me strength to continue being a fighter in life; I really need you. I want you to transform my dark days into light because I feel very weak right now. Please Lord, I am showing you my kids who need a stable life. I am putting my future in your hands. I thank you for letting me finish this year and I ask you to bless my future ahead. I pray all these things in your name. Amen."

Believe me, God works in ways we can't see. We plan our ways. We think that things are impossible, but when God has plans for you, no one can change them. No matter what God you might believe in, I know that with my God, prayers are answered.

One weekend in the middle of January, my best friend Yvette and her two sons –Prince and Thijs – came to visit me in Belgium. The entire year of 2011 had passed without seeing each other, and her kids had missed my children a lot.

Yvette came to Belgium from the Netherlands on a Friday. We spent all that night talking. I told her how I was suffering, that it hurt to hear people talking behind my back, saying that I was desperate and had failed. I cried as I spoke, and she comforted me. She told me she was there to be a shoulder for me to cry on, and she wiped away my tears.

The next day, on Saturday evening, Yvette and I went to visit two of her cousins who lived in Brussels. She wanted to take me out to relax a bit. There I met the boyfriend of one of Yvette's cousins. He was called Lolo.

After dinner, we had some drinks and started chatting in the living room. In the middle of a conversation, one of Yvette's cousins asked if I was getting used to life in Belgium. I told her that I hated it. She asked me why, and I told her the whole story of losing my first job, and not having enough working hours in my second job as a care supporter. Then Lolo intervened.

"Why not go to England?"

I thought I had misunderstood, so I asked him to repeat what he had just said.

"Come and try England. You might get a job and it might also be better for your kids to grow up in an English environment. If you want help, just ask me how things work, because I am living now in England."

I rubbed my eyes at the thought of moving yet again to another country.

"But I've heard England is a very expensive country," I said.

"Have you ever been there?" Lolo asked. "Don't go to London, because when people hear England, they think of London and of course London is an expensive city. If you have someone you know who lives out of London, go there. Just try."

I knew that my sister had moved to Manchester, but I didn't want to put another heavy load on her shoulders because she was separating from her husband and going through a lot at the time.

Yet, my life had been getting hard and harder in Belgium. The landlord had given me a deadline to leave his house because I had failed to pay the rent. My brother was going through a tough time too; he was splitting up with his girlfriend.

England? I asked myself.

I had never prayed that much when I had left all the other countries I had lived in, but this time I really put the pressure on God and told him I needed to know if that was the plan he had for me.

We spent all night chatting with Yvette, her cousins and Lolo, until the first light of dawn. It was 6 a.m. and we were still awake. A few hours later, Lolo drove me and Yvette back to my place.

Give it a Try!

I thought I would simply close my eyes and fall asleep, but I just couldn't stop thinking about moving to England. The kids were enjoying a sleepover at my brother's place. Yvette was enjoying her beauty sleep. It took me ages to get to sleep, even though my place was quiet. When I did, I slept until 3 p.m.

I didn't tell Yvette I was thinking of moving to England, because when I had moved to Belgium, she felt left alone in the Netherlands because we were always together as best friends. Her son Prince was devastated too, because he spent so much time with my kids. The only person I told was my brother when I went to pick up my kids. That same afternoon, Yvette went back to the Netherlands. The next day was Monday and her boys needed to go back to school.

When I told my brother, he was supportive. "Why not? Go for it! Try it and see. I know you are a fighter and you will make it."

My uncle Ismael was living in England near Sheffield, so I decided to call him and tell him that I wanted to move and that I needed his help. I told him that I wanted to go and see how life was in Sheffield. He told me that I was a true fighter and he said that he would send me the money for the tickets.

A few days later, I called a meeting with my kids. My daughter was going to be 12 in two months. My son was 7.

"We are moving," I said.

"What? Moving again?" my son asked. He looked like he wanted to cry. In stark contrast, my daughter remained calm.

"Where to?" she asked.

"England."

"England?" my daughter said. "Are we going to move to Auntie Annie's?"

"No, Auntie Annie lives in Manchester. We are moving near Sheffield, which is a few hours away from her."

"If we move to England," my daughter continued, "will that mean you stop crying all night?"

I was shocked.

"Me? Crying?"

"You cry sometimes when you are sleeping," my daughter said.

I had never cried in front of my children, but I didn't know that I was so heartbroken I could even cry in my dreams. Deep down, however, I knew she was right. I used to wake up in the morning and find my pillows wet, and I would go to look at myself in the mirror and find my eyes were red.

In my daughter's mind, moving was just fine because she was tired of hearing me cry. With my son, it was different. He didn't want to change school and leave his friends.

"Look," I said. "I'll go ahead and see what life's like in England. Then I'll come back and tell you."

Moving to England

I started planning for my journey. I bought the ticket, then in the middle of February, I travelled to a place near Sheffield called Rotherham. I spent a week at my uncle's house and visited places around Rotherham. I asked for information about moving to the UK as a European citizen. I asked about schools for the kids. I went from store to store to look at the prices, especially food. Then I spoke to my uncle.

"I am going to give it a try and come to England."

My uncle offered to host us at his place when we moved.

A week later, I returned to Belgium and told my kids we were moving the following month, in March.

I was still working eight hours a week, so I told Erik that I was going to stop. He was very understanding because he knew I was suffering. I went to my kid's school and informed them that we were heading to England the following month. The headteacher wished me good luck because she could see how I was struggling, but she said she was proud of me that I had kept encouraging my kids to go to school, and that my children had always had the necessary equipment for their classes.

I told my brother that I was moving, as well as my best friends Yvette and Liliane. Yvette was devastated to hear that I was going even further away from the Netherlands, but she understood and said that she always wanted the best for me, adding that she prayed that I would find happiness and a stable life for myself and the kids.

I moved out from my house before I could be thrown out. I then went to my brother's place and waited until I had sorted everything out.

Then, in March 2012, my children and I moved to England.

Chapter 14
STARTING A NEW LIFE

The first week I was in Rotherham, I simply wanted to relax my mind and breathe in the English air. My uncle ran his business full-time – Monday to Sunday – so he had no time to show me around. I trusted myself to do that.

My kids were Dutch-speaking by now and they needed to go to school. I didn't want them to struggle with English at school, nor to blame me for moving them to a country where they didn't know the language very well. I needed to come up with a good strategy for them.

I spoke quite good English and knew that I could help them learn the language. So, one day, I talked to my uncle and asked him if he could do me a favour and help me financially. I told him I wanted to put my kids into various activities, so they could meet other children, and learn to speak with them. He was very supportive.

I entered my kids into swimming, football, and Scouts clubs, so they had three activities each week. Then, I started looking for a job. In England, employers are very serious about asking for references from former jobs. The trouble was, I had no work experience in the UK, so it became very difficult.

Lolo, who had advised me to move to the UK, had told me about the job centres where I could ask for benefits while I looked for work, but before I applied for that, I wanted to try to get a job.

That proved hard, so I signed up for Jobseeker's Allowance – the financial support the government gives to people looking for a job. By the grace of God, they accepted my request for support. That was the first step.

Then, I found a house to rent and the council helped me fund that too by giving me an allowance. The second step was complete. Now I was ready to face the challenges of starting a new life in the United Kingdom.

To begin with, my uncle helped me buy a few items of equipment for the house. I was hoping to get a job very soon, so that I could furnish my home bit by bit. We had moved into a house in Wath-upon-Dearne and my children were now getting used to life in the UK. In September, they all went to school. That was the third very important step – my kids getting into an English school.

Soon they began to feel settled and happy. Indeed, I remember one time when my children asked me, "Mama why didn't we come to live in England a long time ago?" I felt as if my prayers had been answered when I heard that. I couldn't stop crying tears of joy.

Developing a Big Heart

Whenever I moved from one place to another, I would always let Father Aloyz know, so I sent him a message. When he wrote back, he told me that he was busy as a project manager for the construction of a new school – Loyola Jesuit Secondary School in Kasungu, Malawi. He included pictures showing how the building work was progressing.

That message touched me deeply. I sent him a reply saying that I wanted to contribute something when the school started in 2015. I told him that I appreciated everything he had done for me. He had given me a chance in life by sponsoring my scholarship. I really wanted to give something back and help pay for scholarships for some girls. His message back was breathtakingly touching:

Dear Josée,

You are amazing. Here you are, a young mother, two kids, school expenses, worries of life, being alone, and all the rest upon your shoulders! Still, you like to remember that when you yourself were in need, there was help coming to you through my poor self, and now you want to help me to help others... What a wonderful person you are, to have recognized and been grateful for the few tokens of assistance I managed to offer you. Now, I see the depth of your character – your deep love and gratitude. Make sure you tell these stories to your children so that they will grow up knowing that they had a very generous and a good mother, who had some good friends in her life, and she learned from them that one day she could give back and help those who are less fortunate than herself.

Thanks for your great desire to be helpful in what I am doing.

May God bless you, your children and all your dear friends.

Greet your sister and brother and anyone else that I might still remember.

God bless you.

Father Aloyz

Making a difference to those in need doesn't start with a big bank account. It starts with a big heart. If I hadn't had Father Aloyz to help me with my education when I was still a teenager, I could have ended up a miserable person, unable to fight for my rights. No matter how small your help is, trust me: if you have a big heart, you will change someone's life and that person will always be thankful.

Thinking Outside the Box

After a year in Rotherham without a job, I made the decision to move to a big city. Reading online, it was clear there were more jobs to be found in cities. I registered at Sheffield College for administration course and after six weeks, I was awarded a certificate. I decided to do another eight weeks training in health and social work and I also got a certificate for that. This time I felt more confident to apply for more jobs, especially since one of my teachers had given me permission to write his name down as a reference.

On 23 December 2013, I decided to move to Oldham, near Manchester. It took about two months before my kids found new schools. The minute they started, I began job-hunting in the Manchester area. I filled in online applications, walked into hotels, restaurants, and care homes, but there were no jobs. I kept myself busy doing different training courses in security, shop assistance, and other things. I read a lot of books to improve my English, because sometimes I would mix Dutch and English.

Then, one morning in the summer of 2014, I woke up with the idea of doing something which would keep me busy until I could get a job. That's when I started writing this book. It took me one year to write the whole story.

In the summer of 2015, the government stopped supporting me with Jobseeker's Allowance. They said I was an EU citizen and I wasn't allowed to stay on welfare for more than two years. I appealed against the decision, proving that I was looking for a job, showing all my training certificates, but still the answer came back that I had to find a job. Once again, I struggled to feed my kids and pay the rent.

One morning, I went to meet my career advisor who was helping me find a job. After a long conversation, he asked if I had considered starting my own business and becoming self-employed.

"Your personality suits managing a business," he said.

"Is it possible in England to have your own business as a non-British citizen?" I asked.

"Of course. Do you have any ideas for a business?"

I told him that I had one already and that I even had a business plan in my mind.

"Bring your business plan next week and I will have a look at it," he said.

A week later, I went to meet my career advisor with a business plan for selling women's jewellery and accessories. My career advisor looked at it, and without hesitating, he immediately arranged for me to enrol on a business plan training course. "This is a very good business plan," he said. "I don't know why you have wasted your time looking for a job. You could have become self-employed long ago."

"I had no idea it was that easy," I said. "Starting a business in the Netherlands is much more difficult."

"It's all right," he said. "This is the right time."
From that moment, I decided to be my own boss.

Helping Others

In April 2016, I started a charity called *Girls with Pride and Dignity*[1]. This supports young girls who come from less fortunate backgrounds and who miss school because of a lack of feminine sanitary products during their monthly period. It is for girls across the globe. I am the chief executive and the founder.

When the organization started, we thought the problem of girls missing school was only in poorer nations, but in 2017 we found out that in England there were families on low incomes who couldn't afford sanitary products, and that some girls were skipping school during their monthly period. We started providing sanitary products to the Food Banks in the Manchester area, and to other organizations dealing with homeless women.

Even if I have gone through ups and downs in England, at least I have found a stable place where I do what I feel passionate about. My kids have settled and love their lives in England. England is my stable home, but it's hard to call it my permanent home yet. Who knows what's going to happen next?

The Story of a Survivor

I have shared the story of my life, including my adventures, with all the risks I took. I have lived a

---

1 www.gpd-foundation.org

happy life. I have had some dark days and nights. I have made some decisions that have opened doors, and others that have put me in danger, but I believe we are characterized by our weaknesses as well as our strengths, and we shouldn't let what we can't do hold us back from what we could have done.

These are lessons I have learned. Stopping my studies halfway through because I had to run from danger prevented me from finding the career of my dreams. I had a dream from a young age of being a journalist, but because I didn't attain that goal, this didn't stop me finding something else to do. And maybe, in the end, this book is a kind of journalism – a journal of the life of someone who has endured much.

The knowledge that I gained from my education, is what has helped me sit down and write this book. I have had to put all my energy and brainpower into it. For me, writing my own book has been living the dream of being a journalist. I have told you the story of how I became a war victim, a domestic violence victim, how I travelled the world from country to country, how I never got a chance to know my country of origin. All these things may seem to you to have been setbacks, but in fact, they have been the raw materials that have been used to form my personality – the one, constant thing that has helped me to get to the place I wanted to be.

I hope my personality has shone through on every page of this book.

It is the personality of a champion survivor!

ACKNOWLEDGEMENTS

When I finished writing this book, I was not sure if I really wanted to publish it and let the whole world know about my life. I was scared because I didn't think that I had a good story to tell. I was hesitating whether to publish it or to keep it for my close friends and family who would be interested to know about the story they didn't know about me. One day when I was editing my book on my computer, a friend of mine, Mariette, read a bit of what I was writing.

"Wow… girl," she said, "you need to publish this book

"Do you think people would be interested in reading my story?" I asked

"Of course. Your story is amazing and better than the books you read. There are people out there who are interested in reading autobiography books, just like you do"

So, this is for you who finished reading this entire book. THANK YOU so much!

I would first like to thank my Heavenly Father for his blessings. If it wasn't for his protection and love, I wouldn't be alive today.

Special thanks to my dear father, Etienne Kana (who is now in heaven; may you rest in peace and keep watching over us). Thank you for your unconditional love and for your encouragement and inspiration. Thank you for making me who I am now. You are my hero and I miss you very much.

To my mother, Jacqueline Bampangeze, thank you for carrying me for nine months and bringing me up with unconditional love. May God keep protecting you. I love you so dearly.

To my two siblings, Kana Annie Nikiza and Kana Lambert Matsiko. What would I be without you guys? Thanks for caring about me. Your love and support are unconditional. I wouldn't make it in life without you. I love you so much; you are my sunshine.

To my dear brother Kana Deo Ndikumana. May you rest in everlasting peace and thanks for watching over us. I love you so much.

To my children, Lee Ann and Lenny. Thanks for your patience and support with every step we take in life. You are my sunshine. May God bless and protect you.

To Yvette Umutangana, Liliane Narame, Henriette Uwamwezi, Marie Louise Dushimiyimana, Liliane Umuvyeyi, Christine Kanakuze, Theophile Sesonga, Claudette Rwarahoze, John Sidney Varney, Alain Rwanyagasore, Lorrys Munderere, Patrick Robert Misigaro, Mariette Lo, Alex Mvuka, Ange Kabanda, Brune Irankunda, Roy Mwesige, Tatiana Irakoze. Thanks for supporting me through this journey called life. You all mean a lot to me. May you all be blessed.

To Father Aloyz Podgrajsek. Thanks for giving me the chance to continue my education. Without you, I would have ended up in a miserable place. May God bless you.

To John Van Leuwen, Theo Van Lagen, and your families. Thanks for giving me and my siblings a chance in life. To thank you won't be enough. Asking God to protect and bless you would be better.

To Lee-Anne de la Hunt, Patricia Norris, and Claudine Paulsen. You have been a blessing to me during my time living in Cape Town and I can't thank you enough either. May God bless you.

To Gilbert Masengesho, thanks for listening to my story and giving me the inspiration to write about my life. If it wasn't for you, this book would not exist.

To my editors, Mark Stibbe and his wife Cherith Stibbe. Thank you for helping me bring this book to life. This book would not have been possible without your amazing work.

To Samuel Usengimana. Thank you for the implacable work you did with the illustration for the front cover of the book. Your unique drawing of me is the exact image of what I intended it to be in order to help communicate my story.

To Grosvenor House Publishing. None of this would be possible without the hard work of your extraordinary team. Thank you for the great contribution to make my dream a reality.

Special thanks to Melanie Bartle for guiding me through every step to bring my work to one piece. You are amazing!

Milton Keynes UK
Ingram Content Group UK Ltd.
UKHW041514300124
436968UK00001B/19